Printed in the United Kingdom by MPG Books Ltd, Bodmin

Published by SMT, an imprint of Sanctuary Publishing Limited, Sanctuary House, 45-53 Sinclair Road, London W14 0NS, United Kingdom

www.sanctuarypublishing.com

ISBN: 1-86074-270-X

# basic Effects
# & Processors

Paul White

smt

Also by Paul White and available from Sanctuary Publishing:

*Creative Recording 1 – Effects And Processors (second edition)*
*Creative Recording 2 – Microphones, Acoustics, Soundproofing*
  *And Monitoring (second edition)*
*Home Recording Made Easy (second edition)*
*EMERGENCY! First Aid For Home Recording*
*MIDI For The Technophobe (second edition)*
*Recording And Production Techniques (second edition)*


Also by Paul White in this series:

*basic Digital Recording*
*basic Home Studio Design*
*basic Live Sound*
*basic Mastering*
*basic Microphones*
*basic MIDI*
*basic Mixers*
*basic Mixing Techniques*
*basic Multitracking*
*basic Sampling*
*basic VST Effects*
*basic VST Instruments*

# CONTENTS

# INTRODUCTION

Effects and signal processing are important elements in contemporary music production, yet even cheap units can be complicated to understand and operate. For example, rather than produce dedicated reverb units, most manufacturers prefer to build multi-effects units, on which all models (except the cheapest) feature real-time MIDI parameter controls as well as sophisticated effects generation.

Signal processing has also become available as software plug-ins for computer audio sequencers, workstations and even digital mixing consoles. Furthermore, virtually all digital instruments and soundcards include their own effects.

In this book you'll find in-depth explanations of the all of the mainstream studio effects and signal processing treatments, along with valuable tips on how to use them in music production. Once you've seen how these devices work, you'll discover how to patch them in to your system and use them to record and mix creatively.

# 1 EFFECTS AND THE MIXING CONSOLE

Studio effects are designed to enhance recordings, not to compensate for poor playing or imperfect recording techniques. Properly used, however, they can add a new dimension to a good recording. Today effects come as stand-alone boxes – they're built into MIDI instruments, they come as part of all-in-one digital recording workstations and they also exist as software plug-ins for use with computer-based audio workstations and sequencers. Before you can start to use an effect, however, you'll need to know where to connect it in the signal path. To do this properly, it's important that you know your way around a mixing console, especially the aux sends/returns and insert points. The function of these is covered in the book *basic Mixers*, also in this series.

## Auxiliaries

Both adding effects and setting up the performer's cue monitoring can be handled by using what are known as the mixer's auxiliary controls. Figure 1.1

# Effects And The Mixing Console

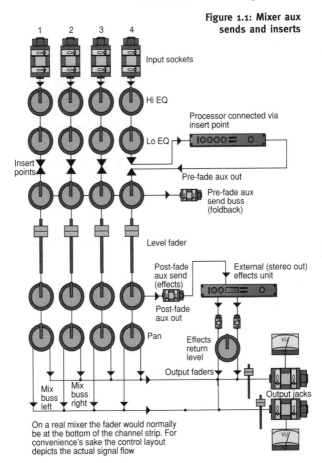

On a real mixer the fader would normally
be at the bottom of the channel strip. For
convenience's sake the control layout
depicts the actual signal flow

13

## basic Effects & Processors

illustrates how these work, picturing a mixer with one post-fade auxiliary send and channel insert points. Effects are invariably fed from post-fade aux sends, which means that the signal sent to the effects unit is also controlled by the channel fader. As the setting of a channel fader is changed during the course of a mix the amount of effect should generally be changed by exactly the same amount, thus maintaining the correct balance of effect to dry signal. This can be achieved by using a post-fade aux send to drive the effects box. If the effects were fed from a pre-fade send, which is independent of the channel fader setting, the effect level would remain the same regardless of the fader setting. For example, if reverb were added to a guitar in this way, and the level was then faded to zero on the mixer, the reverb would remain at a fixed level, even when the dry guitar had been faded to silence.

By using the different settings of the post-fade aux 2 control on each individual channel, it is possible to send different amounts of each channel's signal to the same effects unit. When the output from this effect unit is added to the main stereo mix, adjusting the aux 2 controls on the individual channels allows different amounts of the same effect to be added to the various channel signals.

# Wet And Dry

It's important to note that an effects unit used in conjunction with a channel aux send should generally be set up so that it produces only the effected sound and none of the original. This is usually accomplished by a mix control, which is either in the form of a physical knob or accessed via the effects unit's editing software. The effect-only sound is often known as the wet sound, so the mix should be set to 100% effect, 0% dry.

The output of the effect unit could simply be fed back into the mixer via any spare input channels, but you'll often find dedicated effects return inputs – also known as aux returns – provided for that purpose. Aux returns are electrically similar to the input channels but usually with far simpler facilities: they have no mic inputs, little or no EQ and few (if any) aux sends of their own. Normally they feed straight into the main stereo mix, though on more elaborate consoles it may also be possible to feed them to other destinations.

If a spare input channel is used to feed an effect output into the mix, ensure that the corresponding aux send is turned down on the channel used as a return or the effect signal will be fed back on itself, resulting in an unpleasant howl.

# Stereo Effects

As the majority of effects units have stereo outputs, they need to be connected to either two spare input channels (usually panned hard left and right) or to a stereo aux return input. Figure 1.1 shows an external effects unit connected to the stereo aux return and the two inputs feeding the left and right stereo mix busses. It is usually possible to use just one of the effect outputs to feed into a single channel or return if mixer inputs are in short supply, but the effects will then be in mono only.

However, note that, although the controls shown in the diagrams are arranged logically to illustrate signal flow through the channel, commercial mixers tend to have pan and aux controls located above the channel fader, as the fader is the control most often needing adjustment.

# Insert Points

There is another standard way to connect an effects unit or signal processor to a mixer: via an insert point. All but the most basic analogue mixers have insert points on the input channels and also on the master stereo outputs, though digital mixers may have more limited insert capabilities. An insert point is simply a means of breaking into a signal path at some point so that the signal can be diverted via the external effect or processor device. On most of the analogue mixers you are likely to encounter, the insert points will be in the form of TRS (Tip, Ring Sleeve) jack sockets, which means that you will need a specially wired Y-lead or adaptor to be able to use them. The TRS socket is conventionally wired tip send/ring return. In Figure 1.1 the insert points are depicted by black arrowheads which show their position in the signal path – the sockets actually contain sprung contacts that maintain the signal flow when no plug is inserted.

# Effects And Processors

While it is permissible to connect any type of effect or signal processor via an insert point, there are restrictions on what can be used via the aux send/return system. As a rule of thumb, only delay-based effects such as reverb, echo, chorus, phasing, flanging and pitch shifting should be connected via the aux system, and these are generally called effects. If the box uses delay to do its work it's an effect, and if there's a dry/effect mix knob or parameter the box is almost certain to be an effect. The unique thing about an effect is that it's added to the original signal. A process, such as EQ, doesn't add to the original signal but instead changes the original signal. Processors include compressors, gates and EQ, and are normally only connected via insert points, not via the aux sends and returns. There are workarounds to specific problems that can involve connecting processors to the aux send system, but for all normal operations these basic rules must be observed.

On most mixers there are insert points in the groups and master outs, as well as for the channels, all of which may be used to connect signal processors or effects. If it's necessary to process a group, the group insert points are the only way in. For instance, you might need to compress a stereo backing vocal mix, or even a drum mix, which means using a stereo compressor patched into a group pair. If this is the case, don't forget to set the compressor to Stereo Link mode.

If you want to compress or process a line-level signal in some other way, the obvious thing to do is to patch in the processor via the channel insert points.

# Effects Routing Checklist

- Insert points are invariably presented as stereo jacks wired to carry both the send and return signal, so if you don't have a patchbay you'll need a Y-lead with a stereo jack on one end and two mono jacks on the other. These can be obtained commercially if you don't like soldering.

- Processors must be used in line with a signal and not in the effects send/return loop.

- Most processors work at line level, so you can't plug a mic directly into them. The correct way to compress a mic signal, for example, is to patch the compressor into the insert point of the mixer channel, which comes after the mic amp stage. This doesn't apply to mic channel processors that combine a mic amp with one or more processors.

- If an effect is used via the aux/send return system it's normal to set the effects unit's dry/effect balance to effect only in order to allow the console's aux send controls to determine the effect balance.

- If an effect is used via an insert point it's normal to use the unit's dry/effect balance to control effect balance.

- Some effects, such as phasing and flanging, rely on a precise effect/dry balance, which may be better accomplished in the effects unit itself. In this case, either patch the effects unit into an insert point, or, if you must use the aux/send system, you can either de-route the channel from the stereo mix to kill the dry signal or feed the effects unit from a pre-fade send and turn the channel fader right down.

- To use a mono in/stereo out effects unit via insert

points, simply route one output of the unit to the insert return of the channel feeding it and the other to the insert return of a free adjacent channel. Match the levels, and then pan one track hard left and the other hard right for maximum stereo effect.

- To use a stereo in/stereo out effects unit via insert points, use two adjacent mixer channels panned hard left and right.

- To treat a whole mix with EQ or compression, patch your processor into the master insert points. This places your unit in the signal path before the master stereo faders, which means that, if you're using a compressor, it won't try to fight you if you perform a fade-out. Also, noise generated by the processor will be faded as you pull the faders down.

- If you don't have master insert points you can patch a processor between the mixer's stereo out and the input to your stereo mastering recorder. However, if you want to perform fades with a compressor patched in, you'll need to use the input level control on the mastering machine rather than the one on the desk. You'll also need to monitor the output of the master recorder to hear the effect of the fade.

# Digital Mixers

Digital consoles don't have the same space restrictions as analogue mixers; many of the controls are accessed one at a time by means of a data-entry knob, or the single row of faders can control all of the channel levels, all of the aux send levels, all of the group output levels and so on. Having four bands of fully parametric EQ on both the monitor and input channels is not uncommon, and you may find the same facilities on the effects returns.

Digital mixers perform essentially the same function as their analogue counterparts. The primary practical difference is in the user interface, and the digital mixer is also less flexible when connecting to external analogue devices. There may also be a digital link between the mixer and compatible digital multitrack machines, which preserves signal integrity and simplifies wiring.

Because digital mixers can incorporate more features than analogue consoles, it would be impractical to provide a physical control for each function. Instead there is usually a physical fader for each channel, which is often motorised on automated mixers, but only one set of EQ and aux send controls, or even a single data knob. A selector button by each fader allows the control section to become active for that particular channel, and a display screen usually provides further information as well as a physical representation of some of the virtual controls.

Most digital consoles feature effects, dynamic processing and the ability to automate complete mixes, right down to EQ and aux settings, making it possible to recall an old mix many months later and call it up exactly as it was. However, as mentioned earlier, it's impractical to fit analogue insert points on every channel of a digital console, which is one reason why gates and compressors are usually included. In some situations it may be better to feed the digital multitrack back into the mixer via analogue inputs so that effects and processors can be inserted between them when required during mixing. This procedure is most easily achieved if the recorder is connected to the mixer via a patchbay.

# Optimum Effects Connections

The usual method of connecting a reverb unit or some other effect is to feed it from a post-fade effects send on the console (effectively mono) and then feed the two reverb outputs back into the mixer, either through two effects returns panned left and right or through a pair of spare input channels. The output mix parameter or control of the effects unit is then set for effect only, with no dry signal. If input channels are used as returns, the corresponding aux send must be turned off completely on those channels or some of the reverb will be fed back to its own input, causing feedback of tonal coloration.

To make sure that your reverb unit or multi-effects processor works as quietly as possible, the aux sends on the channels you want to effect should be set to around three quarters full up. The aux send master should also be set at this level – the input level control on the effects unit itself is used to set the signal level entering the unit so that a healthy meter reading can be obtained. The effects unit's output level should be set almost at maximum and the effects return level on the mixer adjusted to provide the right effect level. Following this procedure will ensure that the gain structure of both your mixer and your effects unit has been properly optimised.

You should also turn down effects sends and deactivate mixer channels that aren't being used in the mix. This doesn't just mean turning the fader down – you should also turn off the channel if it has a Mute button, and if you're using a console with routing buttons then make sure unused channels aren't routed to the main stereo mix. It's not often realised that a muted channel with the fader turned down can still add a little noise, known as mix buss noise, just by being connected to the stereo mix buss, so always unroute any channels you're not using.

Processors are generally connected via a console's channel or group insert points, though both effects and processors can be connected directly in line between a line-level signal source and a mixer input if preferred. It is important, however, to realise that most outboard equipment only works properly with line level inputs, rather than with microphone signals. The only exception to this rule is for equipment that includes a mic pre-amp, such as a dedicated voice channel or vocal processor.

Under no circumstances should you attempt to connect the speaker output of an amplifier directly into the input of a mixing console or signal processor. If it's necessary to extract a manageable signal from a speaker output, as may be the case when direct injecting a guitar or bass to preserve the sound of the amplifier, then a purpose-made DI box must be used to match the signal levels.

## Patching And Patchbays

Regularly used inputs and outputs are often wired to a patchbay so that they can be conveniently patched together with short signal leads. Professional patchbays use highly reliable miniature Bantam jack plugs and sockets, often with gold-plated contacts to provide a flexible and durable but highly expensive patching system. Budget semi-professional systems are much more realistically priced and are usually based on readily available mass-produced plastic sockets which accept standard quarter-inch instrument-style jack plugs. Both unbalanced and balanced versions are available. This is a convenient format for the recording musician, as most musical instruments rely on quarter-inch jack connections.

The physical patchbay format usually consists of a rack-mountable 1U panel, generally with two rows of between 16 and 24 sockets, with each socket on the top row paired with the socket below it. Conventionally, the top row of sockets is for outputs and the bottom row for inputs. A typical patching system takes the most commonly used inputs and outputs to the patchbay, where they can be connected as desired using short jack-to-jack leads. Patchbays are most commonly used to gain access to console line inputs, aux sends and returns, equipment inputs and outputs and insert points, but not all are wired in the same way. Any patchbay socket pair wired to handle an insert point must be normalised.

# Normalising

Figure 1.2 shows how the pairs of sockets in an unbalanced patchbay are wired, and the concept is similar for a balanced patchbay. If your console has balanced ins and outs it's sensible to make this part of your patchbay balanced as well, although the insert points on a typical home recording analogue console will invariably be unbalanced. The signal ground connections are often permanently linked between the socket pairs, and there may be a wire or track link on the printed circuit that normalises the two sockets (ie when there is no plug inserted the top and bottom sockets are automatically connected).

Another popular normalising system is to have each pair of sockets mounted on their own separate PCBs (Printed Circuit Boards) with another pair of identically spaced sockets at the back to carry the rear connection. These boards can be easily removed and replaced in one of two orientations, so that either pair of sockets can be at the front. The circuit board is designed so that the sockets are either normalised or not, depending on its orientation.

Normalising is necessary at insert points to maintain the signal flow through the console when nothing is plugged into the insert point, and depending on the

### Figure 1.2: Patchbay wiring

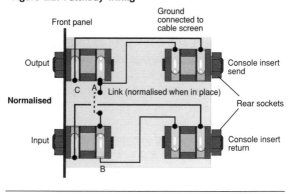

Front panel

Ground connected to cable screen

Output

Console insert send

C · A
**Normalised** · Link (normalised when in place)

Rear sockets

Input

Console insert return

B

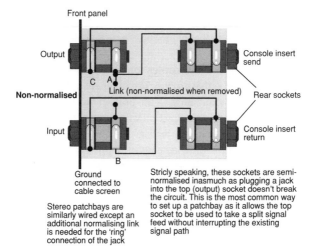

Front panel

Output

Console insert send

C A
**Non-normalised** Link (non-normalised when removed)

Rear sockets

Input

Console insert return

B

Ground connected to cable screen

Stereo patchbays are similarly wired except an additional normalising link is needed for the 'ring' connection of the jack

Strictly speaking, these sockets are semi-normalised inasmuch as plugging a jack into the top (output) socket doesn't break the circuit. This is the most common way to set up a patchbay as it allows the top socket to be used to take a split signal feed without interrupting the existing signal path

27

complexity of the system you may want to normalise other connections, such as the output of your console feeding the input of a DAT machine. This means that your most regularly used signal path is available without the need to insert patch leads, but you can still get at the mixer output or DAT machine input by using patch leads if you necessary.

The most commonly used semi-pro patchbays are fitted with jack sockets on the rear so that they can be easily connected with other parts of the system by means of easily assembled leads. Alternative versions are available that allow cables to be soldered directly onto the rear of the patchbay, and minimising the number of connections in theory produces a cleaner signal path.

In Figure 1.2, contact A carries the signal while contact C provides the signal ground. The other set of contacts, B, is normally found only on the bottom row of sockets and it's this set, in conjunction with the link (shown as a dotted line), which normalises the sockets. Actually, as there is only a switched contact on the lower socket, it would be more correct to say that the patch bay is semi-normalised. What does this mean in practice?

When no plugs are inserted, contact B is mechanically switched to contact A so that the signal which comes in on the back of the top socket is routed via the link to the lower socket, completing the circuit. The console's insert send is routed directly back to its insert return.

If a plug is inserted into the lower socket, the contacts open and no signal flows along the link. If the top socket is patched to the input of an effects device and the bottom socket to the output of the device, however, contact B opens and all of the signal is diverted via the effects unit before being returned to the mixer. You shouldn't fit switch contacts to the top socket because it provides a convenient way of splitting a signal when you want to take a feed from a mixer channel without breaking the normal signal flow. Without a patchbay of this kind you would need a splitter box or a split lead, at the very least, to perform this kind of task.

# Ergonomics

Patchbays are also important in locating all of the inputs and outputs of the effects units, console inputs and aux sends and returns where they are conveniently to hand. In fact, any type of audio connection that you might want to access on a regular basis can be brought out to a patchbay. When the patchbay handles simple inputs and outputs rather than insert points the sockets should be un-normalised, or the inputs and outputs of equipment would be joined when no plugs are inserted into the patchbay, and this might cause the equipment to oscillate.

# Side-Chain Inputs

Another handy connection to have in the patchbay is the key or side-chain input, found on the back of some gates and compressors. Most reputable rack-mounted gear is designed to be used in conjunction with a patchbay, so if you haven't got the information you need to bring the key inputs out to your patchbay, don't be afraid to phone the manufacturer or distributor and ask for more details.

# Wiring

Wiring to and from the patchbay should be done with separate screened cables, but for unbalanced insert points not more than a few feet apart you can generally use a twin-cored screened cable, in which the cores carry the incoming and outgoing signals. The screen connection need only be fixed to one of the jacks feeding the patchbay, as the two socket grounds are linked in the patchbay itself. Foil-screened cable works well and is easy to strip and solder, though any high-quality co-axial cable is also fine. On budget recording, equipment console inserts are generally connected via a TRS stereo jack at the mixer end, so this method of wiring is most convenient. Figure 1.3 describes how a typical insert patch point is wired.

# Routing And Patching

The roles of the various signal processors and effects used in audio production are fully described elsewhere in this book, but it's not always obvious where they should be patched into the signal chain to provide the best results.

If you're using a cassette multitracker then you have few options and everything is simple, but if you graduate to a separate multitrack recorder and mixer you will find yourself confronted with aux sends, insert points and mixing consoles with routing systems so advanced that they rival those on professional desks. Even if you've read the rest of this book and know the basic ground rules, there may still sometimes be a better way of doing things if you stop to think about it.

# Lateral Thinking

By thinking carefully about how your system will actually be used, you can usually avoid connecting every single item to a patchbay. For example, many modern mixers are equipped with six or even eight aux send busses, so unless you have more than eight effects units you could opt to permanently wire your effects direct to the

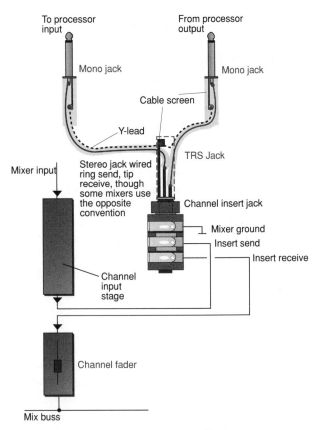

**Figure 1.3: Insert point wiring**

aux sends and returns of your desk. This saves on the amount of patching and money you will need and maintains the best possible signal quality. If you have fewer effects units than sends, you could even wire up the spare sends to a patchbay so that visiting effects could be plugged in.

If your studio is arranged for your own rather than for commercial use, you could permanently plug your favourite vocal compressor into channel one of your console, for example, and then always use this channel to record your lead vocals. If you also make sure that you record your lead vocal onto tape track one during every session you can also bring it back through the same compressor without having to repatch.

The same philosophy can also be applied to gates: if you only ever use them after recording, you could connect them between your multitrack and your desk rather than via the insert points, which would enable you to use balanced wiring (if your gates and tape machine are balanced). This maximises signal quality, reduces the risk of hum and again saves the amount of wiring and patchbays you'll need to use. Of course, you'll have to plan your sessions more carefully so that anything that needs gating is recorded onto the tape tracks that correspond to your gates, but after just a little thought about your own working methods you'll probably find that you can cut the complexity of your patchbay down to around 25% or less of that of a full patchbay system.

The same applies to exciters or enhancers – if you always enhance the whole stereo mix without adding any other overall processing then you can wire your enhancer directly into your console's stereo insert points, but if you prefer to use it on just some parts of a mix and not others then you could wire it into a pair of group inserts instead.

If you're using a mixer that connects via standard jacks and you've made a number of permanent routing decisions similar to those above, you might even be able to do away with the patchbay altogether because, on the rare occasion that you want to set up something out of the ordinary, you can always change the connections to the mixer. This is obviously inconvenient if you have to do it every session, but proves to be less of a problem if you only need to do it once in a while.

I must stress that, if you're looking to set up an efficient patchbay system, you'll have to plan it carefully before you start, and if you decide that you can manage without one you will still have to plan! It's good practice to use a separate patchbay for MIDI signals on DIN connectors, and if you have a collection of vintage analogue voltage-controlled synthesisers then the same applies to gate pulses and control voltages. Mic inputs would normally be routed to a wall box rather than a patchbay, and (if the mixer input is balanced) connected using balanced XLR plugs and sockets.

# 2 EQUALISATION

Equalisers can be either simple bass/treble controls or multiband parametric devices, but equaliser (usually abbreviated EQ) is really just another word for tone control. The limits of human hearing are generally accepted as being around 50Hz–20kHz, so most equalisers affect frequencies within this range.

The simplest equaliser commonly found in audio equipment is the shelving equaliser, a device that applies cut or boost rather like a volume control, but only to the frequencies above or below the cut-off point of the equaliser, depending on whether the equaliser is based around a high-pass or a low-pass filter.

## Shelving Filters

A low-pass shelving filter, as its name suggests, passes all frequencies below its cut-off frequency but affects all frequencies above its cut-off frequency. Similarly, a high-pass filter passes all frequencies above its cut-off frequency but affects all frequencies below it. Figure 2.1 shows the frequency response graphs of a typical

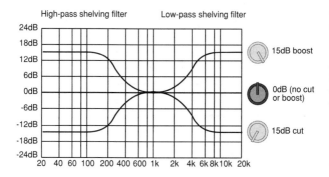

High-pass shelving filter  Low-pass shelving filter

15dB boost

0dB (no cut or boost)

15dB cut

**Figure 2.1: Shelving filter response**

treble/bass equaliser using high- and low-pass filters. Note that the filter graph shows up as a slope at the cut-off point – it isn't possible (or even desirable) to have a filter that does nothing at one frequency and then comes in with full effect after an increase of just 1Hz. Simple shelving filters typically have a 6dB-per-octave slope so that their influence is heard more progressively.

# Bandpass Filters

A filter that passes frequencies between two limits, such as the mid-range controls on many mixers, is known as a bandpass filter. On a typical mixer the bandpass filter will have variable cut and boost, and it will be tunable so that its centre frequency can be

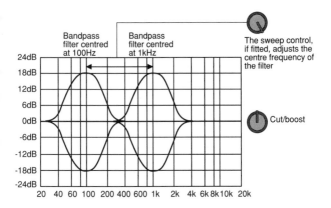

**Figure 2.2: Bandpass filter response**

changed. This is known as a *sweep equaliser* because, although the filter frequency can be changed, the width of the filter cannot. Figure 2.2 shows the response of a typical bandpass filter.

# Parametric EQ

A parametric EQ is very similar to a sweep bandpass EQ, with the exception that a third control is added to allow the width of the filter to be adjusted. The width of a filter is sometimes described as its Q value, where Q is the filter frequency divided by the number of Hertz which the filter affects. Because of the curved nature of the filter response, the actual frequency width is measured between the points on the graph at which the signal level has fallen by 3dB. A high value for Q corresponds to a very narrow filter, whereas a low value of Q corresponds to a wide filter. Higher Q values are useful when it comes to picking out sounds that occupy a very narrow part of the audio spectrum, whereas lower values of Q produce a smoother, more musical sound.

A studio parametric EQ may have several filter sections so that three or four parts of the frequency spectrum can be treated simultaneously. It can be a time-

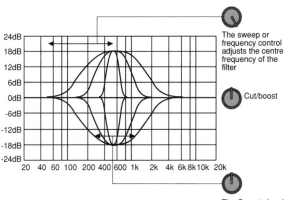

The sweep or frequency control adjusts the centre frequency of the filter

Cut/boost

The Q control varies the bandwidth of the filter. The narrower the bandwidth the higher the Q value

**Figure 2.3: Parametric EQ response**

consuming process to properly set up a parametric EQ, but they are the most powerful and most flexible of all types of equaliser EQ. Figure 2.3 shows the response of a typical parametric equaliser.

# Graphic Equalisers

A graphic equaliser can be recognised by a row of faders across the front panel, each controlling its own narrow section of the audio spectrum. For example, a 30-band graphic equaliser provides independent control over 30 different bands spaced a third of an octave apart.

Other than the highest and lowest faders (which control shelving filters), each of the filters in a graphic equaliser is a fixed-frequency bandpass filter which applies boost in response to the fader moving up from its centre position and which applies cut when the fader is moved down. On a graphic equaliser the range covered by each fader is fixed, and the width of each individual band of a third-octave equaliser is actually rather wider than a third of an octave in order to allow a smooth overlap between bands. Figure 2.4 illustrates the response of typical a graphic equaliser.

# Psychoacoustics Of EQ

Over the past couple of decades, EQ has moved further away from the corrective domain and has joined the

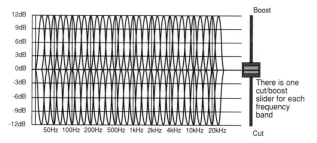

**Figure 2.4: Graphic equaliser response**

more obvious effects boxes as a creative effect in its own right. As well as simple bass and treble 'tone' control, most recording mixers now offer additional mid-band control, often with a variable frequency or sweep function, and more sophisticated systems include parametric EQ, which provides several bands of control where frequency, bandwidth and degree of cut and boost are all adjustable.

EQ can place sounds in perspective if used intelligently, placing lead vocals and solos at the front of a mix, support instruments slightly behind them and sound effects at a distance. A mix is like a painting: if all of the colours are too bright there'll be no way of differentiating between the foreground and the background.

# Spectral Mixing

A lot can be accomplished by using simple hi/lo EQ, but separate controls for the mid range – as in the case of a parametric equaliser – make the equaliser much more flexible. The benefit of a parametric equaliser is that you can tune the equaliser to the fundamental pitch of an instrument and then add boost or cut to change the instrument's apparent level without having too much effect on the sound on either side. If the level of the instrument is then reduced by turning down the gain to restore the original subjective balance, frequencies produced by that instrument that are some distance from the fundamental frequency will also be reduced in volume, which will help to reduce any spectral overlap between sounds that might otherwise be too similar. This is a corrective process rather than a creative one, however, and if you can choose more appropriate sounds at source you'll probably find that the end result is better than using EQ to bend the sounds to fit. Spectral mixing is effective, however, and it's worth experimenting with it to understand its benefits and limitations. It's quite common to remove low end from acoustic guitar parts so that they don't clutter the lower mid range of the mix, where the vocals also happen to be located.

# Loudness Curves

While a good hi-fi amp has a perfectly flat frequency

response, the frequency response of the human hearing system is nowhere near as flat. What's more, the perceived changes in frequency response depend on the level of the sound being heard so that we hear more low end and more top end as a sound gets louder, but the mid range become progressively more recessed. A graph depicting frequency response shows a curve with a dip in the centre – often known as a smile curve – which deepens with the loudness of the sound. The Loudness button on a stereo system emulates this smile curve so that material can be played back at low volume yet still convey some impression of loudness.

In the studio you can create a similar effect by pulling down the mid EQ and then increasing the overall level to compensate. Pulling down the mid range can also help to make a mix appear less cluttered, because a lot of the information that's clamouring for attention resides in the upper mid range. Using this knowledge you could, for example, EQ an entire rhythm section to make it sound louder, and then overlay this with conventionally EQ'd vocals and solo instruments. It's easy to make a mix sound louder by cranking up the monitors so that it actually does increase in volume, but there's more skill in making a mix sound loud and powerful regardless of the level at which the playback is set.

# EQ For Positioning

You can use the EQ to help reinforce a natural sense of perspective; most people try to achieve perspective by controlling level (everyone knows that the loudness of sounds decreases with distance), but you can also roll off a little top to consolidate the illusion. Equally, if you want a sound to seem closer, add a little more high-end EQ.

# EQ Cut

In most instances, the final sound will end up more natural if you use less EQ boost, so rather than adding lots of top to vulnerable sounds, such as vocals, in order to get them to stand out at the front of the mix, you should try being more restrained in your use of EQ and instead use high-end cut on factors such as low-level pad sounds, backing vocals and anything else which plays a subordinate role in the mix. This is particularly relevant if you don't have access to a really sweet-sounding, up-market equaliser; most console EQs can sound a little unsubtle if they're used in anything but moderation. Every recording has to be treated on its own merits, but if you're unfamiliar with the use of equalisers it can be difficult to know where to start. For this reason I've included a few notes covering various types of sound and the EQ ranges that might be appropriate to them.

# Bass Instruments

The lowest note on an amplified electric bass guitar is 41Hz, but the higher notes contain significant energy right up to 2–3kHz. Likewise, the traditional pipe organ goes an octave lower, down to 20Hz, where sounds are felt rather than heard. The organ's high notes may generate significant energy at the 8kHz mark and beyond.

# Bass Guitars

During the '60s the bass guitar was used to provide little more than a low-frequency pulse, and its sound was invariably dull when compared with today's bass sounds. The contemporary bass guitar sound, in contrast, is partly a result of changes in the instrument (ie the shift from tape-wound to wire-wound strings), new playing styles and the degree of equalisation that can be applied with a modern bass guitar amplification system.

Boosting at around 80Hz can pull out the low bass, while boosting between 500Hz and 800Hz adds a nice aggressive bite. Applying boost at higher frequencies tends to bring out the finger noise and very little else, so if you're after a bright sound, its worth trying to obtain a sound as close as possible to what you're looking for before adding EQ. Playing technique is an important factor in the tone of a bass guitar, and no amount of EQ will compensate for a feeble-fingered playing.

A touch of low-mid cut at around 200–250Hz can sometimes be effective when combined with a little low-end boost, warming up the low bass end without causing the low mid area to become uncontrollably boomy.

# Bass Synths

Bass synths can be treated in much the same way, although their ability to produce higher harmonics means that EQ applied at higher frequencies will also prove effective. You should be cautious when using very bright bass synth sounds, however, as they can easily fill up all of the space in a mix, leaving the result sounding congested.

# Electric Guitars

The electric guitar is not a 'natural' instrument, so anything you want to do with it using EQ is acceptable if it works on an artistic level. If you need to add warmth to the sound of an electric guitar then concentrate on the area between 125Hz and 200Hz. There's no point adding boost much below this region, however, as the lowest note's fundamental frequency is 82Hz. Bass boost will therefore only bring up the cabinet boom and make the overall sound appear muddy; it could also conflict with the bass guitar. Equally important is the fact that boosting the bass end will accentuate any mains hum in the signal (most guitar pick-ups, especially single-coil versions, pick up a surprising amount of hum).

Attack can be added to the sound at the 2–4kHz region of the audio spectrum, but there's no point in adding any really high-end boost unless the guitar is DI'd because there's not much coming out of a guitar speaker above 3–4kHz. All you'll do is bring up the background noise, and if the guitar is being used with an overdrive sound this can sound buzzy or fizzy.

In a congested mix two similar-sounding electric guitars can be separated by adding bite at different frequencies – one at 3kHz and one at 4kHz, for example. However, this is rarely as successful as obtaining a different sound at source. It will help if you can use two different amps or pre-amp settings while recording the two parts, and also to use different types of guitar – perhaps one with single-coil pick-ups and one with humbuckers. If you're miking the guitar amp, try using different mics for the different parts – a dynamic for one take and a capacitor for the other will make a noticeable difference, even if guitar, amp and player remain the same.

## Acoustic Guitars

I try to record acoustic guitars with as little EQ as possible, instead moving the mics in order to obtain the right basic tone. Players and producers always seem to want to add more top end, however, and so using some EQ is inevitable. More severe equalisation may be called for if the acoustic guitar is playing rhythm in a pop mix. because the body resonance can clash with the other instruments in the arrangement. In this case the sound can be thinned out by cutting below 200Hz. Boosting in the region of 4–6kHz adds a nice American jangle, but a good guitar with fresh strings is needed to make this work well. You will also need to use a good-quality capacitor microphone, as dynamic mics are insufficiently sensitive and fail to reproduce the high-frequency detail which characterises a good acoustic guitar sound.

# Vocals

Situated a little higher up the spectrum, vocals can range from around 80Hz to 1kHz, depending on the style and sex of the performer. Again, there's a significant amount of energy above that range, which is why manufacturers of live mics often build in a presence peak at 3kHz or 4kHz.

Always use a pop shield when recording vocals because no amount of EQ will fix popping once it's on the tape. General brightening can be achieved by using the shelving high EQ control on the mixer, but listen carefully for sibilance. Boosting lower down, at 1–2kHz, gives a rather honky, cheap sound to the vocals and so is not recommended, except as a special effect. In a mix of backing vocals, rolling off a touch of bass often helps the sound blend in more smoothly with the mix.

# Strings And Brass

Brass and string instruments work on entirely different principles but respond to equalisation in similar ways. Between 1kHz and 3.5kHz the sound can become nasal or honky, but a little subtle cutting in this region can sweeten things up. To add high-end sizzle try adding boost in the 6–10kHz band, but don't overdo it or the sound will become spitty. For a warm pad sound from string or brass samples and synth patches, roll off a little top and add a hint of boost between 300Hz and 400Hz.

# Pianos

You'll need a pair of good mics to record a real piano, but again you can apply the following suggestions to piano samples if they're not already to your liking. Bass end can be warmed up by gently boosting at the 90–150Hz range, while the attack detail can be brought out by bringing up the 4–6kHz section. If the sound is boomy then listen out for the offending area between 250Hz and 350Hz and apply just enough cut to keep it under control.

Because the piano is such a natural and familiar instrument it pays to use less EQ and concentrate instead on positioning suitable mics. Electronic pianos can be equalised in the same way, though many models offer such a range of piano sounds that equalisation may prove quite unnecessary.

# Drums

Drums constitute a special case when it comes to equalisation because the accepted pop and rock drum sound is not that of a natural kit. The trick is to make the drums sound both bright and solid but not to make them too thick.

# Kick Drums

A close-miked bass or kick drum without EQ will often sound less than ideal. It's usually necessary to add definition to the hit, plus a degree of low-frequency weight. For a straightforward punchy sound, a little 80Hz boost will almost always improve matters, but to obtain a deeper sound without the end result being either boomy or stodgy you could try adding 10dB or so of boost with your shelving bass control (most consoles have their bass controls at 50Hz or 60Hz) and then wind in 10dB or so of cut at around 220Hz with the lower mid control. The two controls will work together to produce a narrow area of low-frequency boost, rather than the wide and uncontrollable boost obtained by using only low EQ.

To add definition to the beater impact, try boosting the upper mid range between 3kHz and 6kHz and choose the final setting by ear. Wooden beaters are far better than felt beaters in producing modern kick drum sounds, and the slap can be further enhanced by taping a piece of thin plastic (a piece of credit card, for example) on the drum head at the exact spot that the beater impacts.

## Toms

Toms may be handled in much the same way as bass drums, with boost applied to the 80–120Hz region adding punch and depth. Careful adjustment of the upper mid control can help pick out the stick impact, and if the tom rings on too much or if it rings in sympathy with other drums it's usually possible to roll off quite a lot of low bass without the result sounding thin in the mix.

## Snare Drums

Snare drums are quite unpredictable, and you never quite know how they're going to sound until you've put up a mic and listened to the result over the monitors. The sound can be fattened by boosting the 90–140Hz band, while the bite can usually be located in the 3–7kHz region. When searching for the right area, it's easiest to apply full boost and then tune to find the appropriate pitch. Once you've found it you can then reduce the degree of boost until you arrive at an adequate sound. If the drum still isn't crisp enough then try switching to a capacitor mic.

# Cymbals

Always record cymbals at a low level in order to avoid overloading the tape, and remember that they always cut through in a mix more loudly than you might expect. Brightness can be added with the use of the shelving high EQ control, or you can tune the upper mid control until you find a sweet spot. Cymbals are generally recorded as part of the overhead mic mix, and in some cases it can help to roll off the bass end quite significantly to prevent the drum sounds picked up by the overheads from obstructing the drum sounds from the close mics.

# Summary

Equalisation should always be brought into play after every effort has been made to obtain the right sound at source, and there's a huge subjective difference between the sounds produced by budget and top-quality studio equalisers. Although difficult to quantify, really good equalisers allow you to make more drastic changes without the sound appearing unnatural.

It's also important to understand that the human ear is far less critical of EQ cut than it is of boost, so if you can solve the problem by cutting the area of the spectrum that seems to be too loud then the result will be more natural. A combination of cut and boost is often required, but always use the bypass switch to flip back and forth between the equalised and unequalised sounds to check that you really have improved matters. Equally, when you've EQ'd an instrument in isolation, make sure that the setting you've chosen works in context with the rest of the mix, as parts invariably sound quite different when played alongside other elements of a mix.

# 3 ENHANCERS

Equalisers can be viewed as level controls that work selectively on the harmonics within an audio signal, but there's another kind of device, generically known as an enhancer, which brings about tonal changes by using quite different principles. When an audio signal is subjected to either intentional or accidental distortion, high-frequency harmonics are introduced that were never present in the original signal. Distortion can sound quite unpleasant, but by using filters to confine the distortion to the upper reaches of the audio spectrum it's possible to fill in missing or weak HF (High-Frequency) detail in a manner that the human brain will accept as natural, which is the premise on which harmonic enhancement operates. There may also be a dynamic element to the process by which most harmonic enhancement is applied to transient sounds. This technique achieves an apparent increase in detail, presence and loudness, and is particularly useful in those cases when the original signal doesn't contain enough natural high-frequency components for regular EQ to be effective.

# Dynamic EQ

EQ can only ever work with the material which is already present, so if the frequencies you want to hear never existed in the first place then no amount of EQ will bring them out. Another limitation is that, when you apply conventional EQ, it's there all the time until you switch it off, and so you can't decide to add bass boost only to the kick drum beats, for example, or to add top boost only to the snare hits while leaving the sounds in between untouched. Fortunately, this particular effect can be obtained through the use of dynamic equalisation, which is a combination of EQ and compression arranged in such a way that the amount of tonal boost varies according to the dynamics and spectral content of the signal being processed.

Dynamic equalisation can significantly increased the tonal contrast within the music, something which fixed EQ cannot do unless it's applied only to separate tracks within a mix. Dynamic equalisation is used in several enhancers, and one of the simplest and most effective systems is to set a bandpass filter to between 6kHz and 8kHz, compress the output and then feed a small amount of the compressed signal back in with the original signal.

Commercial enhancers combine elements of dynamic EQ with other processes, including harmonic synthesis and phase manipulation. Not all manufacturers use the same combination of techniques, however, and so as you might expect each type of enhancer has its own characteristic sound.

# Phase Manipulation

One psychoacoustic fact that can be exploited is that, by delaying low-frequency harmonics relative to the higher harmonics, a sound can be given more presence. At least one commercial enhancer works by splitting the audio signal into a number of frequency bands and then applying different delays to each band before recombining them. Low frequencies are delayed the most (by up to 3ms) with higher frequencies receiving proportionally less delay. Frequencies above 1Hz or thereabouts are not generally delayed at all but may instead undergo some form of dynamic processing, such as compression or expansion, and a block diagram of this type of enhancer is shown in Figure 3.1. Because this process emphasises the high end of the mix it sometimes helps to boost the bass end to compensate for this, and so a typical modern enhancer working on the phase-shift principle will have a low-end EQ control as well as a high-frequency enhancement control.

Setting up an enhancer of this kind is fairly straightforward and usually involves adjusting the

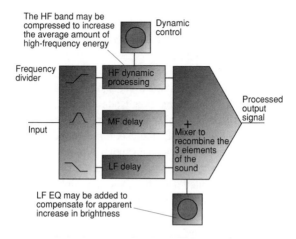

**Figure 3.1: Phase manipulation enhancer**

enhancement control to process the high end to the required extent and then using the low EQ control to make up for any loss at the bass end.

## Harmonics

As stated earlier, a number of commercial enhancers also employ some form of harmonic synthesis, a technique first used commercially by the American company Aphex, who went on to patent the process. Their system creates new high-frequency harmonics that may not have been present in the original recording, but because these harmonics are musically related to the existing mid-range harmonics they sound convincing and natural.

In this process, some of the input signal is diverted into a harmonics generating circuit, via a side-chain and high-pass filter, as shown in Figure 3.2. The high-pass filter may be adjusted by the user from around 2kHz to over 6kHz, and the side-chain signal is fed into a non-linear circuit where the new harmonics are created with a form of controlled distortion, and where phase shifts are introduced by the high-pass filter. Some compression is applied to the harmonics generator output before the treated signal is fed back into the original signal path.

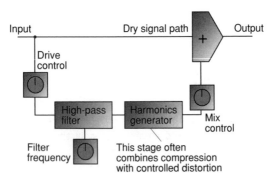

**Figure 3.2: Harmonic enhancer**

Only a very small amount of the processed signal needs to be mixed back in with the original to create the desired effect, but, like the phase manipulation system described earlier, the process doesn't affect the low end of the spectrum and so low-end EQ or other types of low-frequency enhancement may also be applied to help produce a better-balanced sound.

# Setting Up Harmonic Enhancers

On basic models the user may first have to adjust a drive control to ensure that the correct signal level is being passed to the circuitry which generates the harmonics. Some newer models avoid the need for drive adjustment, in which case the main controls are the filter and the mix knobs. Careful adjustment of the filter circuit is essential, as this determines where in the audio spectrum the new harmonics will be introduced. In a full stereo mix it may only be necessary to add a little brightness to the top end of the cymbals or to add a little breathiness to a voice, while if you're treating a solitary snare drum you may want to affect more of the spectrum, in which case the filter could be set to a lower frequency.

Most units, if not all, will have a bypass switch which, when thrown, will allow the processed signal to be directly compared with the untreated sound, and also a mix control which will blend a small proportion of the harmonically enriched signal with the original untreated signal. The enhancer should be regarded as a processor and connected in line with the signal (usually via an insert point).

When setting up the equipment, advancing the mix or enhancement control so that the effect becomes obviously excessive will enable you to hear the effect of the filter control on the new harmonics. Once this has been determined, the mix control may then be turned down so that only the necessary degree of enhancement is added. If a stereo signal is being processed then both channels should be set in an identical fashion. (Enhancers don't usually have Stereo Link modes.)

# Where To Enhance?

Although they are often used to treat individual tracks during mixing, harmonic enhancers are also useful when used in mastering or post-production situations. When treating production master tapes for use in cassette duplication, for example, high-frequency enhancement can help to compensate for the loss of clarity inevitable in the mass-duplication of cassettes. The process can also be helpful, to a lesser extent, in adding life to a master tape that has been mixed on inaccurate monitors or to an analogue master tape that has suffered high-end loss because of repeated playing, ageing or because of minor errors caused by misalignment of the heads during recording.

The careful use of enhancement when mixing can help to make specific sounds stand out more clearly in a mix. While it is possible to enhance a complete mix, this will rob you of a valuable opportunity to create contrast by enhancing just those elements of the mix that you want to stand out. Harmonic enhancement may be used to make a lead vocal sound more intimate, but take care to avoid sibilance, because any form of high-frequency enhancement – including conventional EQ – tends to exaggerate this. Harmonic enhancers also work well on poorly defined drum sounds, electric pianos and acoustic guitars.

# Bass Enhancement

High-frequency enhancement makes mixes sound more transparent and detailed, but there's often a need to increase low-frequency punch, especially in rock and dance music. The traditional way to achieve this is with EQ, but a conventional equaliser with a fixed setting may affect sounds that you'd prefer were left alone. The enhancers that use dynamic equalisation to enhance bass frequencies are usually the most effective in this context.

# Subharmonic Synthesis

Another technique is to synthesise subharmonics an octave below the existing bottom end of the signal. A simple way of achieving this is to use a number of bandpass filters between 60Hz and 120Hz, for example, and then to feed the output of each band into an analogue circuit, known as a flip flop, to halve the frequency. The output from the flip flop is a square wave of fixed amplitude, but if this is used to switch the phase of the original bandpass-filtered signal every cycle the result is a waveform that's closely related to the original in both harmonic content and amplitude, with half of the original frequency. By applying more high-cut filtering to smoothe these synthesised subharmonics, and then combining them with the original signal, it's possible to create the impression of very deep bass. Figure 3.3 shows a subharmonic generator with three frequency bands. It's important to be careful when using these devices, however, as the very low frequencies generated may not reproduce well over small loudspeakers and may even damage loudspeakers if used excessively.

# Psychoacoustic Bass

Most domestic hi-fi equipment can't reproduce the lowest fundamental frequencies produced by bass guitars or some electronic sounds, but these sounds are still

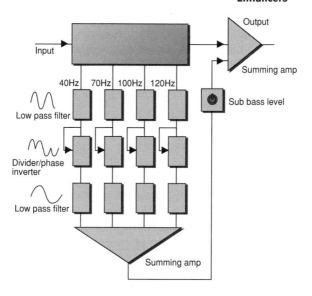

**Figure 3.3: Bass enhancer (boom box)**

punchy because the higher harmonics of the bass sound
are reproduced reasonably accurately and the brain
tends to compensate for the missing fundamental. A
relatively new digital process has been developed,
however, which enhances the apparent bass energy of
sounds destined to be played back through smaller
speaker systems, and this is achieved by extracting the
harmonics from the bottom octave or so of the original

sound and then doubling their frequency. The same system also allows the very low end of the original signal to be lowered in level in order to reduce the stress on small speakers. By reducing the low bass and increasing the level of the newly generated bass harmonics the sound can actually be made to sound as though it has more bass energy when played back over small speakers, even though the low-frequency energy may have decreased. Figure 3.4 shows this process in graphic form. Other techniques may also be used, such as compressing the level of the newly added harmonics.

# Stereo-Width Enhancers

There's also another type of enhancer designed to increase the subjective stereo width of a mix in order to create the illusion that some sounds in the mix come from points outside the speakers. The simplest way of achieving this is to use a trick employed by ghetto-blaster-type portable stereo systems and stereo TV sets to make the speakers sound further apart than they really are. All you need to do is to take some of the right-hand signal, invert its phase and feed it into the left-hand channel. Similarly, some of the left hand signal must be phase inverted and fed into the right-hand channel. The resulting effect is a subjective widening of the speakers. However, if you go too far in separating the stereo width the mix develops a hole in the middle

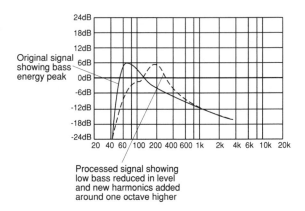

**Figure 3.4: Bass harmonics generator**

as sounds panned to the centre cancel each other out. Used with caution, however, this trick works quite well, and it's also perfectly mono compatible as all of the phase-inverted sounds cancel each other out and disappear when the sound is switched to mono.

There are, however, far more sophisticated ways of increasing stereo width. The best-known commercial 3D enhancement systems are probably Q Sound, Roland's RSS system and Spatializer, all of which work in similar ways but which were developed by using quite different methods. We hear and identify sounds as coming from all directions, including up and down, with only two ears. This is achieved by our brains measuring the slight time delay between sounds arriving at one ear and then the other to help estimate the direction from which the sound is coming. If a sound is directly in front, behind, above or below us the sound will arrive at both ears simultaneously, and the difference in arrival time of the sound will be the greatest when the sound source is directly to our left or right.

Taken on its own, the difference in arrival time at which the sounds enter our ears is not enough to determine the exact point of origin, but there are two other effects that provide the brain with vital clues. Firstly, the head itself casts a kind of acoustic shadow, so if a sound is directly to our left it will arrive at the right ear not only a fraction of a second later but also lower in level and with a lower high-frequency content because of the masking effect caused by the human head.

We have the shape of the outer ear to thank for the second effect because it acts as mechanical equaliser, with different response depending on the angle at which the sound approaches the ear. Similarly, the EQ of the outer ear changes as the sound source moves from below to above the head. By using these principles as a guide, it should be possible for us to build a kind of 3D joystick that duplicates the inter-ear delay and simulates the EQ effects of both the masking of the head and the polar response of the outer ears in order to emulate a natural sound arriving from any direction. But before we can successfully approach this there's one more factor to be considered.

When we hear a sound over conventional speakers the right ear hears some sound from the left speaker, and vice versa. By calculating the level and spectral shape of this crosstalk it's possible to create a signal that cancels it out. Even so, systems which use this approach can never be entirely successful because not everyone has the same domestic listening conditions and the outer ears of different people have different polar frequency characteristics. Realistically, these systems can position some sounds outside the speakers very convincingly, but they work better on some types of sound than others. Because the results can be unpredictable, it's generally best to treat only specific elements within the mix, such as incidental percussion and synth stings. There are currently a number of hardware and software processors available for the purposes of stereo width enhancement, and the most cost-effective of these are software plug-ins.

# 4 COMPRESSORS AND LIMITERS

Pop music production often involves controlling the dynamic range of both instruments and vocals to a high degree, where dynamic range is taken to mean the range between the loudest and the quietest sounds. The processor used to control this dynamic range is the compressor. Traditionally an analogue device, the compressor now has counterparts based on digital hardware and software plug-ins, all of which nevertheless work in much the same way. The effect of dynamic range reduction brought about by the use of one of these devices is known as compression. It's probably fair to say that, after a reverb unit, a compressor is the most important signal-processing tool in the studio.

Compression can be used on any sound that needs to be limited in dynamic range, but it is used most commonly on vocals. Not only is an untrained singer's voice likely to fluctuate in level quite considerably without compression but compression also has the effect of making a sound seem more solid and 'up front'.

# Gain Control

Before compressors were widely available, manual 'gain riding' was employed to keep signal levels under control. This meant that the mixing engineer had to move the level faders manually in an attempt to keep the signal at the right level. As engineers can't see into the future any corrections they make are likely to be slightly late. Figure 4.1 illustrates how the ear follows the signal level from the loudspeaker, thus enabling the brain to direct the hand, which moves the fader until the level is corrected. Looking at gain riding helps us to understand how a machine might perform the same task.

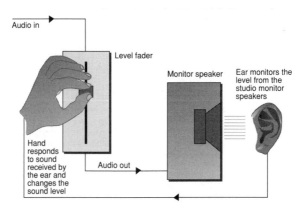

**Figure 4.1: Manual gain riding**

# Electronic Gain Control

A compressor works in much the same way as our gain-riding engineer, in that it constantly monitors the signal level and then makes the necessary adjustments. However, it carries out corrections much more quickly and precisely. Figure 4.2 shows the block diagram of a simple compressor and, as can be seen, it closely resembles the method used by our studio engineer, with the exception that the output signal is

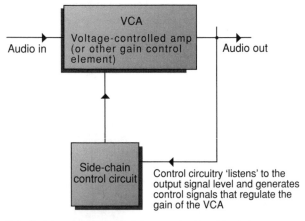

Note that, in some designs of compressor, the side chain monitors the input signal level, but in this version the block diagram more accurately reflects the gain-riding model

**Figure 4.2: Block diagram of a simple compressor**

monitored before it reaches the loudspeaker. The monitoring part of the circuit generates a control signal that continually adjusts the gain of a variable-gain amplifier, thus controlling the dynamic range of the input signal. In practice an electronic compressor can be designed to work by monitoring its own output, its own input or a mixture of both, but to keep this example simple I've shown a compressor that monitors only its own output. The element which exercises gain control may be a voltage-controlled amplifier, a lamp and photocell, a valve, or some form of digital algorithm. Although all of these produce slightly different subjective results, the underlying principle of their operation is the same.

Compressors operate by reducing the levels of signals that exceed a predetermined level. In effect, they turn down signals that are too loud. Most compressors operate on a user-adjustable threshold system, in that signals lower than the threshold remain unaffected while those exceeding the threshold are turned down. The threshold is generally adjusted by operating a front-panel control, and there is usually some kind of meter display to indicate how much gain reduction is taking place, and the amount of gain reduction that occurs when the signal level exceeds the threshold level depends on something called compression ratio.

# Compression Ratio

This ratio is simply the change in output level that results from a given change in input level. A compression ratio of 2:1, for example, means that a 2dB change in input level will only give a 1dB change in output level. The ratio is often determined by the user, so that you'd set a higher ratio if you needed to apply a higher level of gain reduction. If the ratio is set at around 10:1 or greater then this is a situation known as limiting, in which an input exceeding the threshold level is subjected to such a high level of gain reduction that the output is effectively prevented from rising above the threshold level by any significant degree. Absolute limiting (ie where the output never exceeds the threshold value at all) requires a ratio of infinity:1, but in practice ratios greater than around 10:1 have much the same effect (and of course this is assuming that the compressor/limiter can respond quickly enough to catch sudden signal peaks). Most compressors have a wide enough ratio range that they can double as either compressors or limiters. Figure 4.3 shows how the input and output levels of a compressor are affected by the threshold action and by the compression ratio.

Limiting almost always has an audible effect on the sound being treated, unless the amount of gain reduction is kept to a minimum by setting a high

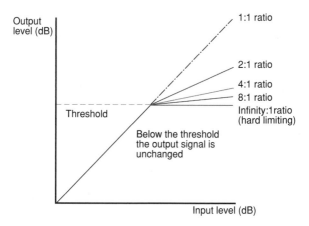

**Figure 4.3: Threshold and compression ratio**

threshold. In most cases a limiter will be set so that it only operates on high signal peaks, so for most of the time it will do nothing. Limiters are often used in conjunction with digital recorders, when there is absolutely no headroom above 0dB FS (0dB Full Scale).

## Attack Time

The time taken for a compressor to respond to a signal that has exceeded the threshold is called the attack time, and some compressors also include an auto mode that adjusts the attack time depending on the characteristics of the incoming signal. The compressor's release time (ie the time that the compressor takes to return to its normal level of gain once the signal has fallen below the threshold) is again commonly linked to a front-panel control, and again this may also be handled automatically by an auto mode.

The attack and decay times are designed to be variable because their optimum setting depends on the type of material being processed. For example, a powerful bass drum beat in a complete mix will cause the compressor to reduce the gain of everything in the mix and not just the bass drum. As a result, any high-frequency low-level detail, such as a hi-hat being played at the same time, will also be turned down by the compressor, leading to a dulling of the overall sound.

One way around this – apart from using as little compression as is practical – is to increase the attack time slightly so that the compressor doesn't respond instantly. In this case, the leading edge of the beat – including the attack of the hi-hat – is allowed through at full level before the gain is pulled down. Some designers also use a high-pass filter to route a little of the high-frequency end of the input material past the compressor without it experiencing a reduction in gain. The setting of a longer attack time is also used extensively in recording bass drums or bass guitars in order to allow the initial click or slap to come through strongly.

If a compressor is used in this way the signal may briefly exceed what you consider to be a safe operating level for a brief instant, but any distortion caused by overloading analogue tape is unlikely to be audible on such short-duration sounds. With digital recording, it is common practice to use a limiter after the compressor to catch any brief peaks that might otherwise slip through, and a number of commercial compressors also include a separate fast-acting limiter.

# Release

The setting of the release time is also important. If it is too short the compressor gain recovers too quickly, with the result that there is an audible 'pumping' or 'breathing' as the gain rapidly changes. Conversely, if the release time is too long, the gain may not have recovered by the time the next quiet sound comes along, which may then be suppressed more than necessary.

# Make-Up Gain

Because a compressor reduces the levels of signals exceeding the threshold, the peak output level will usually be lower that the input level. Extra 'make-up' gain is therefore normally provided so that the output level can be matched to any subsequent pieces of equipment. Along with gain-reduction metering, a compressor may also include further metering to show the input and output levels. Figure 4.4 shows a typical control layout.

## Side-Chain Characteristics

The way that a compressor performs is largely due to the part of the circuitry that monitors the level of the signal being processed: the side chain. Not all side chains have the same response curve, and opto-compressors have particularly complex characteristics that just happen to sound very musical. An RMS, or averaging, side chain responds to sounds in much the same way that a human engineer would: human hearing

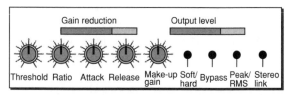

Note: the stereo link switch would only be fitted if either the unit had two linkable channels or if there was provision to link two mono units. Only one channel is shown in this figure

**Figure 4.4: Typical compressor layout**

tends to average out peaks in levels so that sounds of short duration appear to be quieter than sounds of longer duration but the same level. Short, high-level peaks can pass through an RMS compressor unchecked, even if a very fast attack time is set.

Peak-sensing side-chain circuitry isn't caught out by brief transients, and so the compressor is much less likely to overshoot on drums or other percussive sounds unless a long attack time is chosen. To offer the best of both worlds some modern compressors have switchable RMS or peak sensing, and as a general rule peak sensing works better on percussive and RMS on non-percussive sounds.

## Compressor Inserts

The compressor's side-chain normally monitors directly the signal which is being compressed, although an insert point is sometimes fitted, therefore enabling other processors to be connected into the side-chain signal path or allowing the side chain to be fed from a different source altogether. For example, an equaliser could be patched into a side chain to create a vocal de-esser.

By boosting signals in the 5–8kHz range using an external equaliser, the compressor can be induced to respond mainly to sibilant sounds in the that range, and Figure

## basic Effects & Processors

4.5 shows how this works. If 10dB of boost were applied in this range, the compressor would therefore be 10dB more sensitive to sibilant frequencies than to the rest of the audio spectrum, and so most gain reduction would occur when sibilant sounds were present.

## Ducking

Access to the side chain is also required when it proves necessary to enable the level of one signal to control

**Figure 4.5: Patch for full-band de-essing**

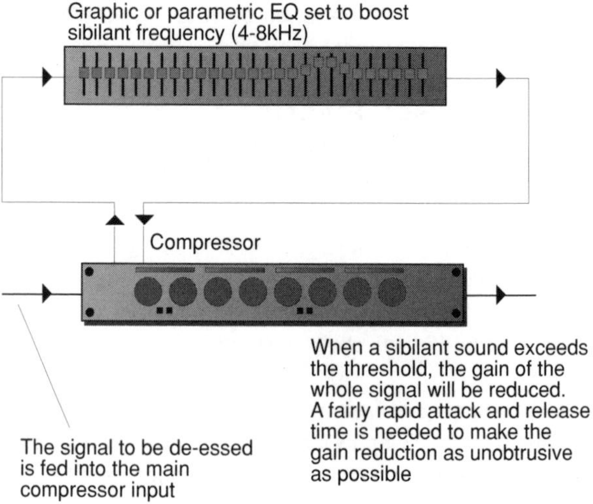

Graphic or parametric EQ set to boost sibilant frequency (4-8kHz)

Compressor

When a sibilant sound exceeds the threshold, the gain of the whole signal will be reduced. A fairly rapid attack and release time is needed to make the gain reduction as unobtrusive as possible

The signal to be de-essed is fed into the main compressor input another. By feeding music through a compressor and connecting a voice input to the side chain the music can be reduced in volume to make way for a voice over. In this instance, when the voice stops the music returns to its previous level, with the rate of return determined by the release control. This technique, often used by DJs, is called ducking. To achieve the effect you will need a mixer which has a mic channel with a direct output or an insert send to feed the compressor's side chain, because the side-chain input on most compressors will only accept line-level signals. The mic signal must therefore be amplified before it can be used. Figure 4.6 shows a suitable arrangement for ducking.

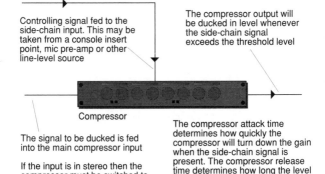

Controlling signal fed to the side-chain input. This may be taken from a console insert point, mic pre-amp or other line-level source

The compressor output will be ducked in level whenever the side-chain signal exceeds the threshold level

Compressor

The signal to be ducked is fed into the main compressor input

If the input is in stereo then the compressor must be switched to Stereo Link mode and both channels must be used

The compressor attack time determines how quickly the compressor will turn down the gain when the side-chain signal is present. The compressor release time determines how long the level takes to rise back to normal once the controlling signal stops

**Figure 4.6: Ducking set-up**

# Soft Or Hard Knee

What happens when the input signal reaches the threshold depends on whether the compressor has a hard- or soft-knee characteristic (Figure 4.7 shows why the term 'soft knee' is used.) With a soft-knee compressor some compression may be applied to all signals, regardless of level, but the compression ratio starts off very low and then increases as the signal level increases. Sometimes there's no ratio control at all, which makes for a very simple compressor set-up as the only knob you need to adjust controls the amount of compression. More commonly, however, there will be both threshold and ratio controls, as there would be for a conventional hard-knee compressor, but in this case the compression ratio will still increase progressively as the signal approaches the threshold. The idea behind soft-knee compression is to obtain a gentler transition between signals that are not compressed and higher level signals that are compressed. As a rule soft-knee compression sounds less obtrusive than hard-knee compression, but you may not be able to exercise such firm gain control.

# Built-In Gates

Because a compressor can't differentiate between a small signal that you want and a low level of noise that you don't, it may end up emphasising such noise by

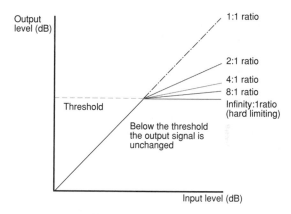

**Figure 4.7: Soft- and hard-knee compression**

setting itself to maximum gain during quiet passages, such as gaps between words or phrases in a vocal track. Including a simple gate or expander before the compressor helps to avoid this problem.

# Stereo Linking

Two-channel compressors designed for stereo use include a stereo link switch. What's needed is for both channels to undergo exactly the same amount of gain reduction at all times, regardless of whether the biggest peaks are in the left or right channel. The link circuitry combines the side-chain signals in such a way that the compressor responds to an average of the two channel levels, and often you'll find that, when switched to stereo operation, the compressor can be adjusted by using the controls of only the first channel.

# Connections

In normal use compressors are connected in line with a signal, often via the desk's insert points, not through the auxiliary send system. Remember: a compressor is a processor, not an effect.

The channel insert points should be used to compress individual signals, whereas for compressing submixes, such as drum kits or backing vocals, it may be best to route the channel to a pair of subgroups and place two channels of compression in the subgroup insert points. The compressor should also be set to Stereo Link mode in order to prevent shifts in the stereo image caused by uneven left/right compression.

In order to compress an entire mix, the compressor should be patched in via the console's master stereo insert points. As a general rule, when you're compressing complete mixes it's a good idea to use a low ratio setting of under 1.5 and to set the threshold at a fairly low level so that all but the quietest sounds are then compressed.

# Digital Compressors

There are relatively few stand-alone digital hardware compressors available (other than those that are designed for mastering), though they can be found built into digital mixers or as software plug-ins on digital audio workstations. In theory digital compressors can do just about everything of which analogue compressors are capable, and they also have the additional advantage of being able to delay the signal slightly so that it's possible for the side-chain signal to detect what's coming a fraction of a second before it arrives at the gain-control section. This facility is known as a 'look ahead', and a compressor or limiter equipped with this is facility is therefore able to deal more effectively with signal peaks. In most other respects, software-based digital compressors emulate the controls and parameters of analogue compressors.

# Applications

Compressors are useful for reducing the dynamic range of both signals being recorded onto a multitrack machine and signals being mixed from a multitrack to a master recorder. The only real difference between a compressor and a limiter is in the compression ratio, and there is no hard-and-fast figure that divides the two, although to ensure that no overshoot occurs under any circumstances a dedicated peak limiter is required, as a general-purpose compressor may not respond quickly enough. Don't make the mistake of over-compressing, especially at the recording stage where it can't be undone. Music needs some dynamics!

# Vocals

Both standard ratio and soft-knee compressors work well on vocals, while the hard-knee type produces a more obviously compressed sound. If you're using a hard-knee compressor, select a ratio of around 4:1 to start with and fine tune it by ear. However, you may want to go as high as a ratio of 8:1 for a hard-compressed rock vocal sound.

Because it's generally a bad idea to have a sharp attack on the words in a vocal line, a fairly fast attack time should be used so that gain control starts immediately. A release time of around half a second is usually a good starting point, and little or no hold time is necessary. Alternatively, a long attack time of, say, 50ms and a fast release time of around 100ms will emulate a vintage photo-electric compressor. If your compressor supports both modes, try this in both hard- and soft-knee modes to check out the difference. The required degree of compression depends on the performer, but you should be cautious about applying more than around 10dB of gain reduction.

If the vocalist has a particularly sibilant style, and if changing the type and position of the microphone doesn't cure the problem entirely, then the additional compression employed during the mix can be made 'frequency conscious' to act as a de-esser, as described earlier. Care must be taken, however, to avoid making the processing obvious by overuse: if the vocal starts to sound lispy when de-essing is occurring you should use less gain reduction.

## Acoustic Guitars

Steel-strung acoustic guitars may be given a denser, more even tone through the use of compression, and with the possible exception of attack time the settings should be somewhat similar to those used for vocals. To give the guitar a nice zingy attack, the compressor's attack control should be set to anything from 10ms to 40ms so that the attack of each note or chord will pass through unsuppressed. The release time can be set from 0.1 to 0.5 seconds, depending on the effect you want to achieve, and for a really glassy tone try using an opto-compressor.

## Bass Guitars

To record a bass guitar you can use either a hard-knee or soft-knee compressor set up in much the same way as it would be for an acoustic guitar (ie to emphasise the attack of each note). Here, however, the release time must be adjusted to match the individual's playing style. Slap and pull bass playing may need a lot of compression to keep the level even, and some of the notes could be quite short, so it will be necessary to set the release time as fast as you can without causing the sound to 'pump'. It may also be necessary to increase the compression ratio to 5:1 or more to keep tight control of the louder notes.

# Electric Guitars

The electric guitar is such a versatile instrument that you really have to think about the sound you're looking for before deciding on the compressor settings. For example, a heavily distorted guitar sound tends to have fairly tightly controlled dynamics, due to the characteristics of the distortion circuitry, so little or no extra compression may be necessary. On the other hand, a clean rhythm guitar would need to be treated very much like an acoustic in terms of compressor settings. EQ should be applied before the compressor for a smooth sound or after the compressor for a brighter, more open tone.

If a sustained sound is desired, without undue distortion, the compressor may be used as an artificial sustain device simply by compressing the input heavily, using a fast attack time and a release time of 250ms or so. The ratio can be set anywhere from around 4:1 upwards, depending on the degree of sustain needed, and you may want to apply a level of gain reduction anywhere up to 20dB. As the guitar sound dies away the compressor will increase the gain to compensate, thus creating the sustain effect. If the attack of a note needs a little more emphasis then slow down the compressor attack while listening to the result until the desired effect is achieved.

# Drums

In rock and pop music, drums are often recorded with very little dynamic range and so some compression is normally applied – especially if the player's technique isn't very even. When close miking drums, a good starting point for the ratio might be somewhere in the range of 4:1 to 6:1, then set an attack time of around 10ms to emphasise the start of each beat, and then adjust the release to be faster than the time delay between successive beats, if at all possible (try settings between 20ms and 100ms).

When ambience mics are being used to create a larger-than-life drum sound in a reverberant room, it is common practice to compress the output from these mics to emphasise the natural-room reverb.

# Dedicated Limiters

A dedicated limiter would normally have the fastest-possible response or attack time, and in applications where absolute limiting is vital a clipping circuit may be included to arrest any short-term peaks that are too fast even for the limiter to control. A clipper is far less subtle than a limiter; instead of trying to control the signal level it simply clips off the top of any signal waveforms that attempt to exceed the clipping level. In combination with a fast limiter such periods of clipping would be very short, and research has shown that periods of clipping less than 1ms in duration, or thereabouts, are not audible.

# Dedicated De-essers

Though compressors can be used with an equaliser patched into the side chain for de-essing, a dedicated de-esser generally produces fewer unpleasant side-effects. Sibilance is a high-frequency whistling sound accompanying 'S' and 'T' sounds, and is caused primarily by air passing through the teeth of the speaker or singer. It can also be aggravated by using a very bright-sounding microphone or by compressing the vocal track. A de-esser removes the unpleasant high-frequency sounds whenever they occur without unduly changing the rest of the audio spectrum.

Sibilance generally occurs between 5kHz and 8kHz, so

it's fairly obvious that using a compressor with an equaliser in the side chain to pull down the level of the whole signal is going to have a noticeable effect on the sound, often producing an unpleasant lisping quality. A dedicated de-esser will be designed to attenuate only the frequency band in which sibilance occurs, so there are considerably fewer audible side-effects.

# 5 THE INTRODUCTION OF NOISE

Noise is a problem in all areas of recording, and can be caused by circuit hiss, magnetic tape hiss, digital quantising, poor screening, ground loops and so on. Acoustic noises also cause problems during recording, including rustling sheet music, squeaking chairs, microphone spillage from other instruments, audience noise, wind and traffic.

Once noise has been added to an electrical signal there is no perfect way of removing it, although there are digital processes that are surprisingly effective at significantly reducing the level of random noise. However, it's good practice to assume that any noise you collect along the way is going to be a permanent part of the recording and that all possible steps should be taken to minimise it. This means that you should always optimise gain structure, unroute unused mixer channels and take all other practical measures to reduce noise at the source. Despite your best efforts, some noise will always remain in your signal – it's a fact of physics – but the less there is, the fewer side-effects you'll incur when trying to clean up your recording later.

# Masking Noise

Unless the noise contamination is quite severe the chances are that it will only be obtrusive during quiet sections of the music, as the rest of the time it will be masked by the wanted signal. A complete mix is very difficult to treat because periods of silence are infrequent, but separate tracks within a multitrack recording – a vocal part, for example – generally have some periods of silence, including pauses between words and phrases as well as longer gaps during instrumental passages. If the signal level could be turned down during these pauses, the background hiss would also be turned down without affecting the music. However, to carry this out manually on every track by using faders would be very difficult, even with an automated mixer, so this procedure is performed with an automatic electronic muting device called a gate.

Early gates were based on an electronic switch that was turned on or off according to the input signal level. On a gate there is a threshold set by the user, much like that on a compressor, but on a gate the electronic switch operates to mute the signal when the signal falls below the threshold. A compressor processes

## basic Effects & Processors

signals above the threshold while a gate treats only signals below it. Figure 5.1 illustrates how a gate threshold system operates, and even the most basic gate will have some kind of indicator, such as an LED, to indicate when it's open and closed.

A basic gate can be little more than a simple switch that is either on or off (with no in-between state), but in this case quiet sounds are in danger of being muted along with the noise, and sounds with natural decays are particularly vulnerable to this effect. A more sophisticated kind of gate action is therefore needed.

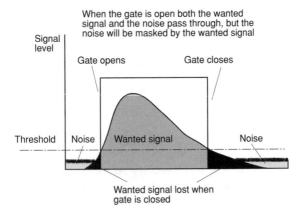

**Figure 5.1: Relationship between attack, release and hold times**

# Attack And Release

To avoid the problem of chopping off low-level sounds, studio gates are fitted with a release-time control so that, instead of simply being switched off when the signal falls below the threshold, the sound is faded out over a period of time set by the user. This represents a dramatic improvement and prevents the noise from being turned on and off too abruptly – an effect which is far more intrusive in most instances than the continuous background noise the gate is trying to hide.

It's also an advantage to include an attack control to determine how long the gate takes to open fully once the input signal exceeds the pre-determined threshold. If the gate opens too quickly, low-frequency sounds may be distorted due to the gate operating partway through a cycle, which can produce an audible click. This problem can be overcome by slowing down the attack time slightly.

On the other hand, a sound like the beat of a snare drum will be robbed of its impact if the gate opens too slowly, so some kind of provision has to be made for very fast operation in these circumstances. At its fastest an attack time of no more than a few tens of a microsecond is desirable, whereas at the slower end several tens of milliseconds might be ideal.

# Range

So far we have investigated threshold, attack and release controls, and in many cases these parameters are all we need, but some units have an extra control called range or attenuation, which allows a certain amount of signal to pass even if the gate is closed. This might be useful during a recording session in which the room ambience is required in the mix, although at a lower level. By using the gate to attenuate this by a few decibels rather than switching it completely the ambience can be allowed through during pauses at a more suitable level. The same is also true for soundtrack recording, where you may be recording a conversation in a busy street and you wish to retain a little street noise for atmosphere, yet at a level that won't interfere with from the main dialogue.

# Hold Time

On some modern gates you also might come across the hold setting. Hold stops the gate entering its release phase for a pre-determined time after the input falls below the threshold. In conjunction with a fast release setting, this can be used to abruptly gate reverb or room ambience in order to create the well-known gated drum sound. A shorter hold setting may be useful to prevent the gate from chattering, which occurs when the input signal constantly fluctuates in level, though selecting a longer release time is also effective against chattering in most circumstances. Figure 5.2 shows how the attack, release and hold times work together.

# Hysteresis

Chattering can be a serious problem when the sound which is being gated has a slowly undulating decay waveform, so the best gates are designed to exhibit a hysteresis effect. Put simply, this means that the signal must fall a few decibels below the threshold at which the gate opens before the gate will start to close again. This has the same outcome as having two thresholds, one for opening the gate and a lower one for closing

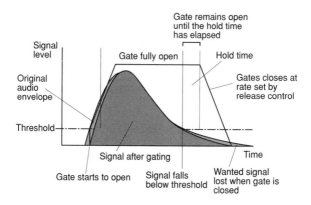

**Figure 5.2: Operation of the threshold system**

it, and in practical terms it means that the input signal has to waver in level by more than the difference between the two thresholds before retriggering can occur. An example of a waveform that might cause problems if the gate did not exhibit hysteresis would be a decaying synth tone with LFO amplitude modulation. Figure 5.3 shows how this type of signal would be handled by gates both without and with hysteresis. The amount of hysteresis is generally fixed and invisible to the user.

## Side Chains

As with the compressor, the gate has a side-chain circuit which measures the level of the incoming signal and compares it to the threshold set by the user. When the threshold is exceeded, the circuit generates a control signal to open the gate at a rate set by the attack control. When the signal falls below the threshold, the gate closes according to the setting of the hold and release controls. Figure 5.4 shows a block diagram of a typical gate.

Like the compressor, a two-channel gate will normally have a linking switch that ensures that both channels switch on and off at the same time when stereo material is being processed, even if the signal is louder in one channel than in the other. Also like the compressor,

**Figure 5.3a: Gate without hysteresis**

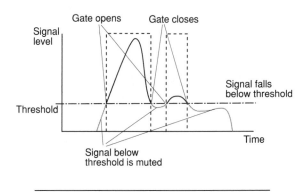

**Figure 5.3b: Gate with hysteresis**

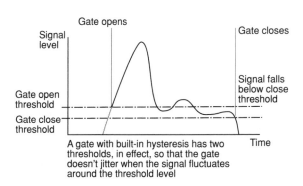

A gate with built-in hysteresis has two thresholds, in effect, so that the gate doesn't jitter when the signal fluctuates around the threshold level

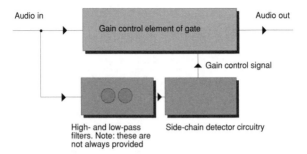

The gate only reacts to the signal that passes through the filter. Note that, as the filters are not connected in line with the gain control element, the audio passing through the gate is not affected by the filters

**Figure 5.4: Block diagram of a typical gate**

this is necessary to prevent the stereo image from shifting, which could occur if both channels were operating independently. In practice, however, there are few applications that require stereo operation, other than that involved in gating the output from a stereo reverb or reverb chamber to create a gated reverb effect.

# External Key Input

For special applications – again, like the compressor – it may be desirable to drive the side-chain from a signal other than that being fed into the gate. To achieve this the gate needs an external side-chain key input; in this way one signal can be used to gate another, and a typical example of this is the bass drum that gates the bass guitar to tighten up the sound. If the bass guitar is played early it won't be allowed to pass through the gate until the bass drum beat occurs. The bass sound will then decay at a rate set by the hold and release controls, so it can be made shorter than the original sound if so desired.

# Gate Ducking

Some gates have a Ducking mode, which enables them to perform the same ducking functions as a compressor. In fact, it can be easier to arrange ducking with a gate rather than a compressor because the range and attenuation controls can be set to determine precisely how many decibels of attenuation are required during ducking. The attack and release times set the speed at which ducking starts and stops and, as with the compressor, the signal controlling the process must be fed into the side-chain key input at line level. The signal being ducked passes through the gate's main signal path in the usual way.

# Side-Chain EQ

Equalisers inserted into the side chain can make the gate respond more readily to some frequencies than to others, and a practical use of such a combination is best illustrated by example. If you're using a snare drum to trigger the gate it's possible that the snare mic will pick up enough of the nearby hi-hat sound to open the gate between snare beats. Using the equaliser to filter out the high-frequency hi-hat from the side chain can significantly reduce this tendency to trigger falsely. Most gates with side-chain access have a Listen switch, which allows you hear the signal feeding the side chain via the gate's output so that you can then set the filter controls by ear and reject sounds that cause triggering problems.

It's common for gates to have built-in side-chain filters so that you don't have to patch in an external one, and these usually take the form of a pair of variable-frequency high- and low-pass filters with fairly sharp cut-off characteristics, usually 12dB per octave. These filters don't directly affect the sound of the output in any way; they only affect the way in which the gate's triggering circuit responds.

## Applications

Of all signal processors the gate is probably that which sounds the most dramatic if set up wrongly. If the threshold is set incorrectly, or if the decay is too short, the sound may be gated on and off in a random manner that can produce an effect like a faulty connection, or even gross distortion. The correct way to set up a gate is to have the threshold as low as possible (without noise causing false triggering to become a problem) and then work on the release time so that the natural decay of the sound being gated isn't affected. Don't set the release time longer than you have to, however, or you'll still hear noise after the wanted sound has died away. The attack time should generally be as fast as possible, but not so fast that audible clicks are heard when the gate opens. Slower attacks can be used as a special effect.

If a signal is hopelessly noisy then it is unreasonable to expect a gate to improve it without introducing unacceptable side-effects, but if you take care with recording levels and minimise noise at source as much as possible then gating can help to turn a good recording into an exceptional one.

## Other Applications

The creative trick of gating reverb on drums is less applicable than it used to be because most digital reverb units now have the effect built in. Nevertheless, it's still used in those cases when the reverb is natural in origin, as with drums recorded in a live room. Here the gate may be triggered via its side chain from the dry drum sound and the ambience mics may be passed through the gate, usually in stereo. The easily recognisable hard-gated drum sound is produced by using a hold time of up to half of a second and very fast attack and release, and Figure 5.5 shows how this might be set up in practice. The effect may be stronger if the ambience signal is heavily compressed before it's gated.

# MIDI Gates

MIDI gates are essentially conventional analogue gates that also output a MIDI Note On message when the gates is open and a Note Off message when the gate closes. This can be useful in a number of creative situations – for example, where a MIDI sound source is used to double up the sound triggering the gate. An example of this might be a kick drum, which is arranged to trigger a kick drum sample at the same time. Recorded drum parts may also be used to trigger samples via a MIDI gate in those cases where it's required to replace the recorded parts with different drum sounds, and Figure 5.6 shows how a MIDI gate may be used to trigger replacement drum sounds.

If you're using a digital-tape- or hard-disk-based recording system it should be possible to offset the drum track so that it occurs slightly early, thus enabling you to compensate for the MIDI delay.

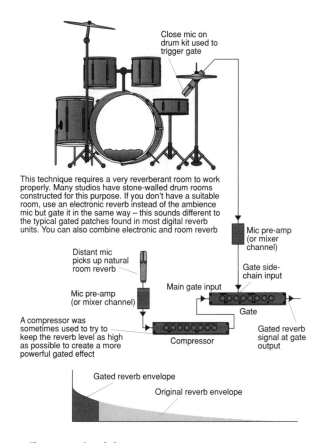

Close mic on drum kit used to trigger gate

This technique requires a very reverberant room to work properly. Many studios have stone-walled drum rooms constructed for this purpose. If you don't have a suitable room, use an electronic reverb instead of the ambience mic but gate it in the same way – this sounds different to the typical gated patches found in most digital reverb units. You can also combine electronic and room reverb

Mic pre-amp (or mixer channel)

Distant mic picks up natural room reverb

Mic pre-amp (or mixer channel)

Gate side-chain input

Main gate input

Gate

A compressor was sometimes used to try to keep the reverb level as high as possible to create a more powerful gated effect

Compressor

Gated reverb signal at gate output

Gated reverb envelope

Original reverb envelope

**Figure 5.5: Gated drums**

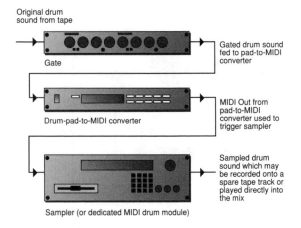

Original drum
sound from tape

Gated drum sound
fed to pad-to-MIDI
converter

Gate

MIDI Out from
pad-to-MIDI
converter used to
trigger sampler

Drum-pad-to-MIDI converter

Sampled drum
sound which may
be recorded onto a
spare tape track or
played directly into
the mix

Sampler (or dedicated MIDI drum module)

Figure 5.6: MIDI gate used for drum replacement

# Expanders

Some gates work on the expander principle, which is
best visualised as being exactly the opposite to that of
a compressor. When a signal falls below the threshold,
instead of it being switched off, as with a simple gate,
it's subjected to gain reduction. For example, if the input
signal was present all the time, at just below the
threshold level, a normal gate would emit no output at
all: it would never open. The expander does emit some
output, however, albeit at a reduced level, and the
further the input falls below the threshold the more the

gain is reduced. For example, a expander ratio of 1:2 would mean that the output would fall by 2dB for every decibel the input fell below the threshold. An expanded signal can sound rather odd, because the peaks are very loud and the quiet sections are all but inaudible, but this expansion only happens below the threshold level, and on sounds less artificial than those produced by simple gating – the signal muting points are less obtrusive, especially if short release times are used.

# Dynamic Noise Filters

Another related device – not a gate in the strictest sense of the word – is the dynamic noise filter, which is sometimes used in combination with an expander or a gate to form a single-ended noise-reduction system. All that single-ended means in this context is that, unlike tape noise-reduction systems (such as Dolby, dbx and so on), the signal doesn't have to be encoded when recorded and decoded on playback. A single-ended system takes any signal, live or recorded, and processes it to reduce the subjective noise content.

A dynamic filter reduces the high-frequency content of the signal being processed as its level drops. To put it simply, as the signal gets quieter the device automatically turns the treble down. This might sound drastic, but as long as you don't use it excessively the reduction in high-frequency noise can be quite dramatic without any apparent loss in brightness. As with most other processors, any side-effects are likely to be less noticeable if individual tracks are processed rather than complete mixes. With care, however, complete mixes can also be improved to a useful extent.

Dynamic filtering works very well because most natural sounds are richer in high-frequency harmonics as they begin, when the amplitude is at its highest, so the filter is wide open at this point, allowing most or all of these harmonics to pass through unattenuated. As the sound decays the high frequencies tend to die away more quickly, and the filtering effect of the dynamic equaliser becomes less obvious. When the input signal falls even further, the expander gate steps in to silence it completely. The expander and filter sections usually have independent threshold controls, and unlike the usual type of gate this system is reasonably effective on complex mixes as well as on individual tracks and instruments.

# Connections

Gates are processors and are always placed in line with the signal being treated, and never via the aux send or return loop (under normal circumstances, at least). Signals may be gated during recording or during mixing, and when gating at the mixing stage you can also gate out any noise that may have accumulated during the recording process. Furthermore, an inappropriate gate setting during recording can ruin an otherwise perfectly good take, whereas an incorrect gate setting at mixdown simply means that you must re-adjust the settings and trying again. However, when several signals are recorded on the same track (as is often the case when recording large drum kits), it may be necessary to apply some gating while recording.

# Digital Noise Reduction

Digital noise-reduction systems, which may be in both hardware and software form, are far more sophisticated than gates or expanders and generally work by first splitting the incoming signal into a large number of separate frequency bands. Some systems may split the audio into over 500 different bands, where each band is equipped with the digital equivalent of its own expander. When the signal within the band falls to a threshold set just above the noise floor, the signal within that band is attenuated. Properly done, this can significantly reduce the side-effects introduced by simple gating or expansion because only those bands in which nothing is happening are attenuated. The signal is unaffected in any band showing activity above the threshold, as is the noise within those bands, but in most cases the wanted signal will mask any noise occurring within the same frequency band.

The trick is to figure out how to set several hundred different thresholds to the right level. Having a common control is fine if the noise spectrum is flat, but in real life the noise energy tends to increase at low frequencies, and with certain sources there may be peaks in the noise spectrum.

Some systems rely on the presence of a short section of background noise and an absence of signal directly before or after the recording of the wanted material. A short section of this noise is selected, usually less than a second in length, and the software is then asked to learn the noise characteristics. In effect, the software performs a spectral analysis of this noise sample.

The information derived from this scan is then used to automatically set the thresholds within the different frequency bands to just above the noise floor, although most systems allow further manual adjustments to be made if required. Most of the time, however, it's only necessary to move the overall threshold up or down by a fixed amount to achieve optimum results. As a rule, computer-based systems have more adjustable parameters than hardware noise-reduction systems.

Although it's possible to completely mute the contents of any frequency band in which the signal has fallen below the threshold, this often produces unpleasant side-effects. Individual filter bands cross through the threshold due to fluctuating noise levels, so when the adjacent bands are muted they tend to ring or chirp at the characteristic frequency of the band, producing an unnatural tinkling sound. This sound occurs at a very low level, but in the absence of noise the effect can be quite disconcerting. A better compromise is reached by attenuating (rather than completely muting) the bands which fall below the threshold, and in most commercial systems this value can be adjusted by the user. In practice a reduction in noise of several decibels is possible with virtually no side-effects, though much depends on the type of material being processed and the sophistication of the noise-reduction algorithm.

# Advanced Digital Systems

The reason why a basic multiband noise-reduction system can bring about only a limited improvement in noise performance without audible side-effects is partly because noise doesn't have a constant spectrum – it may change throughout a recording as noise sources are faded in and out of the mix. Also, because it's statistical in nature, noise is more unpredictable than we'd perhaps like it to be. It's these changes in noise that cause the levels in each band to jitter on either side of the threshold, causing ringing or chirping. Raising the overall threshold may reduce the chirping effect, but other audible side-effects may then become apparent, such as a loss of low-level detail in the signal being processed or a choked, lifeless sound. Advances are constantly being made in this area, however, and even relatively inexpensive systems often include intelligent threshold management systems designed to reduce the magnitude of chirping.

A more advanced approach is to use a system that can mathematically differentiate between noise and wanted signal on a continual basis so that, in effect, the thresholds within the bands are updated several times a second. Such systems don't require an isolated noise sample to analyse, which is an advantage when you're dealing with a master tape on which all of the recordings have been topped and tailed to remove all traces of noise before the starts and after the ends of the tracks. By constantly adapting to the changing noise spectrum these systems are able to provide around twice as much noise reduction before side-effects become apparent.

# De-clicking
This is another process that can be effectively performed in the digital domain. De-clicking is a process designed

to reduce or remove the annoying clicks in a recording that are caused by digital glitching or scratches on records that have been transferred from vinyl to a digital format. De-clickers use elaborate algorithms that analyse the behaviour of the wanted signal and also refer to stored information about the characteristics of clicks and scratches to identify the sections in which problems are occurring. This isn't an easy task, as some naturally occurring sounds can sound very much like clicks, so there's usually some kind of user-adjustable threshold available, as well as a system for auditioning just the information which the system is set to remove. For example, you may be able to audition just the clicks to make sure that no wanted audio material is being mistakenly identified.

The file can be processed once the parameters have been set up. In the case of both de-noisers and de-clickers, slower computers can perform this task when off line while faster machines – or those with DSP assistance – can do the job in real time.

Removing clicks while de-clicking isn't enough, however, as this would leave gaps in the waveform. Part of the program's job is to make an educated guess as to what the missing piece sounds like and then reconstruct it. Although the reconstruction may not be entirely accurate, the additional sounds are usually of such short duration that any momentary increase in distortion is inaudible. At worst there may still be a very low-level click where there was once a loud one!

# Gates And Reverb

It's best to avoid gating a signal that has had reverb added to it if at all possible (unless you want to create deliberate gated reverb effects), as you may chop off some of the reverb decay. It's a much better idea to gate the signal before adding reverb or delay, because then not only will the reverb remain intact regardless of the gate setting but the reverb will also help to disguise any discontinuities in the original signal caused by the gate action.

# Gate Applications

Vocal sounds that are sung usually have a fairly fast attack followed by a slower decay, although some words can cut off abruptly, especially those that end with hard consonants. If the gate is set to open very quickly it's still possible to introduce a click on those words that have a slower attack than others, so if you increase the attack time to one or two milliseconds this will help to reduce the risk of experiencing clicking in general-purpose vocal applications. This is still fast enough to allow the attack of the word to pass through without any of it being lost, but it's also slow enough to avoid audible clicking. In those situations where the background noise is high, resulting in a higher-than-usual threshold setting, it may be necessary to further increase the attack time to avoid clicks. In any event, always listen carefully to ensure that the start of the word isn't being cut off.

A release time of between a quarter and half a second should be enough to avoid truncating the ends of words, yet it should still be fast enough to fade out the noise quickly at the end of an abrupt sound. If noise is still audible after the ends of words, try shortening the gate release time even further. The gate may open and close rapidly on a sustained note that fluctuates in level, resulting in a chattering effect, in which case the hold time should be increased until the chattering stops. If there is no hold parameter then try extending the release time. Chattering is normally only a problem when you're using shorter release times, but if the release time is extended too much in an attempt to alleviate the effect then the sound being gated may end before the gate closes completely, leaving any background noise unmasked. Inevitably, all gate settings are a compromise, and part of an engineer's skill lies in finding the best settings for each particular job.

**basic Effects & Processors**

There's a similar problem with the threshold level: the lower you can set the threshold the less obtrusive the result will be, but if it's set too low there is a danger that background noise or unwanted sounds will trigger the gate. It's therefore important that good recording practice is observed in order to keep noise as low as possible at all stages of the recording process.

If you're compressing vocals at the same time as gating them, it's generally better to insert the gate before the compressor. If the gate kicks in after the compressor, the reduced dynamic range will make it more difficult to set the threshold control correctly.

Other instruments can also be gated, as long as you take care to set the attack and release times to match the characteristics of the instrument. As a rule you should set the attack time of the gate to as fast as possible without incurring clicking and then set the release time to as long as possible without allowing noise to creep back in at the ends of decaying sounds. Also, you should always double check that you're not shortening the decay of a sound by an unnatural amount.

# 6  INTRODUCING EFFECTS

One of the problems encountered when recording in a home studio is that every acoustic instrument you record sounds small or 'dead' because your recording space doesn't have the same degree of acoustic ambience as a concert hall or club. In fact the same is also true of most professional studios, apart from those with large, live rooms, and most pop music is recorded fairly dry, either in a fairly dead environment or by close miking. Electronic effects units are then used to recreate the desired ambience, and by far the most important effects unit of them all is reverberation, or *reverb*.

Reverberation occurs naturally when sound is reflected and re-reflected from walls and other surfaces within a large room, and an electronic reverb unit mimics this effect by generating thousands of reflections electronically. Reverb, like all modern effects, can be used to create the impression of a real room, but it may also be used to create new effects that have no obvious counterpart in nature.

If you record in a dry environment and then add effects during a mix, you can experiment with different types of effect after the recording has been made. Of course this is quite feasible in the professional studio, which may have a big mixer, lots of tracks and plenty of different effects units, but in a small home studio it's often more practical to add some effects as you record and others as you mix.

Basic guitar effects are usually recorded to tape because they affect the way in which the guitarist plays. Even so, it's best to avoid adding reverb until last. Not only does this allow you to find the right type and balance of effects but it also enables you to keep the reverb in stereo, which contributes greatly to a feeling of space and depth within a mix. Effects added when recording will usually be in mono because there simply aren't enough tape tracks to keep everything in stereo, but a little stereo reverb added while mixing provides a surprising amount of depth.

# Reverberation

Reverberation is closely linked with the way in which we perceive sound, and it contains clues which our subconscious uses to determine such things as direction, type of acoustic environment and distance. Because it's a naturally occurring effect, it's important that any electronic emulation sounds as authentic as possible or the human ear will not be fooled.

Reverberation occurs naturally when a sound bounces from the surfaces within a room, and its effect is evident as a series of closely spaced echoes following the original sound. If you were to examine the individual reflections that make up natural reverb you'd discover that, after the initial sound, there's a short pause as the sound travels to the nearest surfaces (wall, floors and ceilings) before then bouncing back to the listener. A great many closely spaced reflections bounce back after this, and some of these encounter other surfaces and are re-reflected.

As time elapses, the complexity of the reflections builds up rapidly so that the individual echoes are no longer audible, and the intensity of the reflections dies away because natural materials absorb sound as well as reflect it. Most materials absorb high frequencies more readily than low frequencies, and so as the reverb decays it sounds increasingly dull. Different types of rooms and different materials produce different sounds, which is why modern reverb units provide a number of different room types and user-adjustable parameters.

Most musical applications require a fairly short reverb

time (between one and three seconds), although digital reverb can also emulate huge caverns with decay times of ten seconds or even more. Plate settings are popular for general use, especially on vocals and drums (the term plate refers to the mechanical reverb plate that was used to obtain the effect before digital reverb units were invented). For practical purposes this decay period – known as the reverberation time of a room – is usually defined as the time taken for the level of the reverberation to decay by 60dB, and is sometimes referred to as the RT60. Some of the sound energy, especially the higher frequencies, is absorbed by the air itself, but this effect can be ignored for most small rooms. However, it's one of the reasons why large buildings produce a warm reverb sound, even if they're made of a hard material, such as stone.

In real life a different pattern of reverb reflections can be heard with each ear, and this provides the brain with stereo information. Even if the sound source is mono – a single voice or hand clap, for example – the reverberation will always be in stereo. In order to produce a convincing stereo effect, digital reverb units process a mono input to produce two different sets of synthetic reflections. Figure 6.1 shows the pattern of decaying reflections created by a typical digital reverb unit.

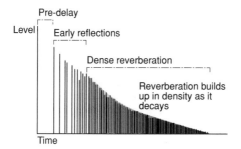

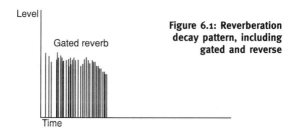

**Figure 6.1: Reverberation decay pattern, including gated and reverse**

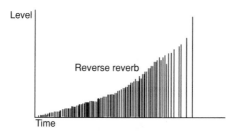

# Digital Reverb

Creating electronic reverb is far more complicated than combining a few digital delay units. Research has shown that somewhere between 1,000 and 3,000 separate echoes are needed every second to create the illusion of dense, natural-sounding reverberation. Additionally, the spacing between these reflections has to be chosen very carefully or the resulting reverberation will ring in a most unnatural fashion.

Obtaining appropriate reflections is only part of the story, however. Digital filtering is needed to impart the right frequency characteristics to the reverberant sound, and the software needs to be sophisticated enough to create a number of different simulated environments without becoming too complicated for the user to set it up. Good digital reverb units can produce excellent approximations of real acoustic spaces, but they also have the capacity to create reverberant characters that simply could not occur in nature. For example, what bizarre set of natural parameters would result in a reverse or gated reverb sound? Gimmicks aside, however, digital systems also allow us to produce reverbs that are longer and brighter than anything normally encountered in the real world.

Those models currently available usually fall into two

types: the fully programmable variety and the less costly preset-based machine, on which there may only be one user-variable parameter per preset.

If we first examine the programmable type it will then be easy to understand the compromises that must be made in a preset machine. Both varieties have stereo outputs and may have either mono or stereo inputs, depending on the manufacturer's preferences. In either case, the reverb is generally derived from a mono mix of the inputs – only the dry signal remains in stereo throughout. This is quite acceptable, in practical terms, because reverb comes from all directions regardless of the stereo positioning of the original sound, and so for natural-sounding reverb a mono in/stereo out system is all that is needed.

However, a number of machines also offer true stereo in/stereo out operation for the production of special effects. Dual Reverb modes are also common, whereby the same processor can function as two independent reverb units where one is fed from the left input and one from the right. These may be mono (in which case the processes are quite separate) or they may be stereo, with the outputs from both virtual reverb processors summed at the output of the unit. This latter mode is useful if a short reverb is needed for drums and a longer one from vocals in a mix. All you need to do is feed the two inputs from different console aux sends. Only one stereo aux return is required for the effects unit.

# Adjustable Parameters

The main reverb parameters available for user control are pre-delay time, early reflection pattern and level, overall decay time and high-frequency damping. Pre-delay simply sets the time between the original sound and the first reflection, and may be variable from virtually instantaneous to half a second or more. This is a simple way of creating the illusion of room size and also helps to separate the dry sound from the reverb. Longer pre-delays can be useful in conjunction with medium-decay vocal reverb to prevent the reverb from clouding the vocals.

Early reflection patterns are not usually variable as such – the user normally makes a selection from a handful of stored patterns simulating various rooms, halls, chambers and plates, or small-room ambience, though in some cases the level and spacing of these reflections is variable. The greater the spacing the larger the room sounds.

Overall decay time simply determines how long the reverb takes to die away, and longer reverb times suggest large environments with very reflective surfaces whereas shorter ones may be used to simulate the natural acoustics of a small room. Most reverb units can produce an impressively long decay time, but the true test of a reverberator is how convincingly it emulates small-room ambience.

High-frequency damping allows the high-frequency decay time to be shorter than the overall decay time in order to simulate the absorbency characteristics of real rooms, simulating the absorption of both surfaces and air. Some units also have independent control over low-frequency damping to simulate environments that reflect mainly high-frequency sounds.

By selecting the appropriate pattern for the environment to be simulated and then adjusting the other parameters, the available effects can vary from a barely reverberant room to a huge cavern, in which the reverb decay thunders on for several tens of seconds. In practice, because excessively long reverb tends to muddy a mix, most of the useful applications of reverb have a decay time below two seconds – although, or course, there are circumstances in which a long reverb can be effective.

Some models incorporate a control which governs the

reverb's room size by adjusting several of the parameters simultaneously to give the impression of a larger or smaller space. This is useful because it means you don't have to manually reprogram several parameters.

# Gated Reverb

In addition to simulating natural reverberation, two further effects have become standard issue in the armoury of modern digital reverb: gated and reverse.

Gated reverb was first created by using the ambience of a live room (often heavily compressed) and a noise gate to produce an abrupt cut-off rather than a smooth decay. The effect is a burst of reverb following the initial sound that persists for half a second or so before ceases abruptly.

Most reverb units provide an electronic emulation of this effect by using a burst of closely spaced reflections that stop abruptly after around half a second. The main parameter in this instance is the gate time, which is in effect the length of the reverb burst following the end of the original sound.

# Reverse Reverb

Reverse reverb does not, as the name might suggest, involve anything actually being playing backwards but is instead achieved by applying a reverse envelope to a group of reflections so that, instead of decaying, it builds up in level after the original sound before cutting off abruptly. Like gated reverb, the main parameter is the time taken for the reverb to build up and cut off.

# Delay

Delay, as the name suggests, is a means of delaying an audio signal to produce one or more distinct echoes, and is the electronic equivalent of the old tape echo unit. A feedback (or regeneration) control adjusts the amount of output signal that is fed back into the input so that repeating echoes can be set up. The feedback gain must be less than 'unity', however, or the echoes will build up in level rather than decay, resulting in an uncontrollable howl.

On some models there is a phase invert switch in the feedback path which triggers a subtle change in sound at very short delay times, particularly with flanging effects. Its use determines whether the flanger cancels or accentuates odd or even harmonics, and the choice of setting is entirely a matter of taste – the higher the level of the feedback the longer the echoes take to decay. The main parameters of this device are delay time and feedback. Figure 6.2 shows a block diagram of a delay unit.

## basic Effects & Processors

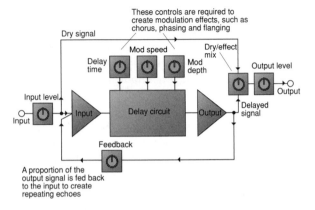

**Figure 6.2: Studio delay unit**

To set up a single delay the depth and rate of modulation and the feedback controls should be set to minimum and the range control adjusted for the length of delay required. You can then use the Fine control to match the delay time to the speed of the song on which you're working – the effect is viable from a short slap-back echo of around 20ms to a distinct repeat occurring a second or more after the original sound. Converting this single repeat into a true repeating echo is simply a matter of advancing the feedback control. The signal at the output is then fed back to the input and so goes through the delay again, with the time taken for the echoes to die away being set by the amount of feedback. With the feedback set at maximum the echoes may go on indefinitely or even build up uncontrollably, so care must be taken when adjusting this control if you're already working near the maximum setting.

## Emulating Tape Echo

The old tape delays had terrible technical specifications but they still produced a wonderfully warm sound, and the limited bandwidth on which they operated was only one reason why. There was also the rather poor stability of the tape transport – musicians would leave their echo units in the van for days, all the time with the rubber pinch roller pressing against the capstan. Often this would impress flats on the pinch roller, resulting in a little unevenness in the transport speed, and so instead of perfectly clean repeats they'd all have a tiny amount of vibrato applied.

This effect can be simulated by inserting a chorus or vibrato block before the DDL (Digital Delay Line), but it's important to keep the effect very subtle or the chorus will be too obvious. With real tape echo, more vibrato is added every time a repeat is fed back and re-recorded, making each repeat less accurate than that before it. To emulate this exactly with a DDL you'd need to put the chorus effect between the feedback loop and the delay line input. Many algorithms don't permit you to do this, however, in which case a little chorus before the DDL will get you close enough.

# Multitapped Delay

Modern multi-effects units often include multitapped delay programs that generate multiple echoes at different delay times. It may also be possible to pan the individual delays from left to right in the stereo field to create interesting spatial effects.

A popular technique involves setting the echo delay time so that the repeats are in time with the tempo of the song, although shorter delays can be used to create a doubling or double-tracking effect.

Echo effects were popular back in the '60s and early '70s, when they were often used on lead guitars and vocals. The effect is still popular today and is used on all types of instrument and voice.

# Using Delay

Simple delay and echo is always popular, both on vocals and instruments, but it's generally considered to be more useful if the effect's delay time is matched to the tempo of the track so that there are one, two or four echoes per bar, or even in such a way to produce triplet measures. In this way the repeats reinforce the beat of the song rather than detracting from it. However, it's possible to experiment with the delay time to create new and more complex rhythms by timing the repeats to occur in unexpected places, especially if you are treating drums or some other percussive sound source.

An often-used trick is the adding of echo to certain words or phrases, usually at the end of lines or verses. This is accomplished by turning up the echo or aux send control just before the phrase occurs and shutting it down again immediately afterwards. However, if you try the same thing by using the effect return level control instead, you'll find that you can't control exactly those which words have echo and those which don't.

# Modulation Effects

Originally conceived as a successor to tape loop echo machines, DDLs soon acquired modulation controls that allowed them to produce a wide range of effects, from echo and doubling to chorus, flanging, ADT, vibrato and phasing. All of these effects are available on a modern multi-effects unit, but it helps to understand how these are created by examining the elements of a dedicated DDL. Indeed, it's surprising how many of the standard studio effects are variations on the principle of digital delay, where the delay time is modulated by a low-frequency oscillator to produce chorus, flanging, phasing and vibrato effects. Modulation in this context simply means that the delay time is varied under the control of a low-frequency oscillator. Some modulation effects, such as phasing, use delay times which are so short that no delay is perceptible, while chorus and ADT use a slightly longer delay time to produce a doubling or thickening effect.

# Chorus And ADT

Chorus uses a short delay of up to around 70ms to create a slight doubling effect, and the delay time is then modulated to produce a slight wavering in pitch. An equal mix of delayed and unprocessed sound is used to produce an effect rather like two instruments playing the same part but with slight differences in timing and tuning. This characteristic of chorus makes it useful for creating ensemble effects from single instruments. The chorus depth is controlled by the modulation depth of the LFO, and as a rule the faster the modulation the less depth required. It is often used on string sounds, synthesiser pads, electric guitars and fretless bass guitars.

ADT (Automatic Double Tracking) is similar to chorus but uses a delay time in excess of 70ms to create a more pronounced doubling or 'slapback' effect, and it uses a shallower depth of modulation. ADT is often used to process vocals in such a way to make it appear that the same singer has performed same the part twice, on different tape tracks. Again, this is done to obtain a thicker sound. The amount of modulation should be so slight as to be only just discernible.

# Flanging

Flanging is essentially similar to phasing, though it may use slightly longer delay times (up to 50ms, for example) and the feedback control is advanced to provide a dramatic, swirling effect. In general terms, you can get away with using more flanging with a slower rate of modulation. With a higher feedback setting the sound becomes more 'whooshy'.

Finding the right effect demands a precise balance between the direct and delayed sounds to create the optimum effect, so it may be as well to experiment first with the channel insert points on your desk rather than the aux sends. Once you've got the hang of it you can try using the aux sends, but it is trickier to get the balance precisely right this way. Again, if you try to arrange it so that the flanged sound (an equal mix of dry and delayed signal) is panned to one side and a dry version of the signal is likewise panned to the other you'll find that the effect is much more dynamic and gives the illusion of movement as the flange sweeps through. This is a useful alternative to the ready-made stereo flanging found on most multi-effects units.

Flanging can be applied to any instrument or voice, but because of its distinctive nature it's not appropriate in all contexts. If a sound is left dry and its reverb send is flanged this can provide a more subtle alternative, and indeed this is used by a number of producers to achieve a shimmering reverb effect. An increase in the amount of feedback applied results in a more aggressive effect.

Some delay effects have a phase invert function that is most noticeable on effects that use a very short delay time, particularly flanging. By inverting the phase of the signal fed back to the input it allows different harmonics to be accentuated by the filtering process, providing a choice of two types of tonal coloration, one usually sounding thinner than the other. The type that you end up using is entirely a matter of personal choice, based on the context of the song on which you're working.

# Phasing

Phasing users shorter delay times than flanging and little or no feedback to produce a moving comb filter which sounds not unlike mild flanging. Because the effect is more subtle than flanging it can be used more extensively, and many '70s records feature phasing on the lead guitar.

## Vibrato

Vibrato is a modulation in pitch similar to that produced manually by guitar and other string players, and is created by using only the delayed sound and none of the original. The delay is kept to just a few milliseconds so that the timing of the performance isn't significantly affected, and the modulation depth sets the vibrato depth.

## Pitch Shifting

Pitch shifters can change the pitch of an original signal without changing the speed of the sound, and they usually have a maximum range of at least one octave up and down. Pitch shifting is often found in the modulation section of multi-effects units, but it isn't a modulated delay process at all. It works by breaking the sound into very short segments and sampling them in turn. Each sample is then either looped or truncated, depending on whether the pitch is being moved up or down, and digital algorithms are used to splice the segments back together in order to avoid glitching. Most low-cost pitch shifters impart a strange timbre to the sound, caused by the regular modulation involved in the looping and splicing processes, but if mixed with the original sound this side-effect can be disguised. Sampling and splicing also causes a short delay, but this can be as short as just a few milliseconds.

Smaller pitch shifts sound very similar to chorus effects, although without the regular modulation of chorus. Such detuning treatments, combined with short delays, are often used to double or thicken vocals. Larger shifts can be used to create octaves or parallel harmonies, and 'intelligent' pitch shifters can be set to add musically correct real-time harmonies to vocal or guitar parts. Interesting effects may also be achieved by pitch shifting percussive sounds to create deep snare and kick drum sounds.

The newest pitch shifting feature is known as formant correction, the idea being that the character of a voice can be changed without altering its speed, or, alternatively, the pitch of a voice can be changed without running into the usual Mickey Mouse effect. It is anticipated that future developments in this area will allow singers to change their voices so that they resemble more closely the voices of the artists they are covering.

## Autopanners

An autopanner is simply a device that automatically pans a mono signal from left to right in mix, usually under the control of a low-frequency oscillator or an external trigger, and used in time with the tempo of a track panning can be quite subtle. Many multi-effects units include a panning facility as well as a rotary speaker emulator, a setting designed to emulate Leslie speakers, which provide a mechanical means of producing a chorus effect by placing rotating baffles in front of the speakers, and similar systems that employ rotating baffles to add vibrato to organ sounds. Most rotary speaker sounds combine panning with chorus, and they often have two speeds, with a delayed accelerate and decelerate function to mimic the mechanical inertia of the real thing.

A basic autopanner would normally be fed into two mixer channels, panned left and right, to make a sound in a mix move back and forth across the soundstage. This was popular in the 1960s, and was much used by artists such as Jimi Hendrix. With a slow pan rate the sound would drift in a leisurely fashion from left to right, while at a higher rate (say 5–10Hz) it might sound a little like a stereo tremolo.

## MIDI Control

A more subtle use for this type of panner is to move an effect such as echo or reverb back and forth while the untreated sound remains in a fixed position. Ideally this movement should be timed to relate to the tempo of the music, but with a simple free-running panner this can only be approximate. A number of multi-effects units include MIDI-controllable panning as one of their effect options, so if you're working alongside a MIDI sequencer it should be possible to use MIDI clock to synchronise the pan rate to the tempo of your track, even if the sequence includes tempo changes. Most MIDI sources, such as synths and samplers, may also be panned automatically using MIDI controller data.

# Programmable Effects

Virtually all but the very cheapest digital effects units are now programmable and offer MIDI control over patch selection as well as some form of dynamic MIDI control over the effect parameters. Programmability allows the user to set up several effects of each type, and with chorus, flanging, ADT, vibrato and other delay-based effects, the programs, once created, will probably be useful in a number of different contexts, with little or no further modification. Pure delay, on the other hand, often needs to be fine tuned, simply because a lot of delay effects are related to tempo. Various delays can be stored to suit all of the more popular tempi, but a more satisfactory solution is to use the 'tap tempo' facility now found on the majority of effects devices. With this the user taps the tempo of the song on a front-panel button or footswitch, and the delay time automatically matches itself to this tempo. It is only necessary to tap twice, but if the song contains tempo changes then these can be tapped in at the appropriate places.

A typical programmable reverb or multi-effects unit provides a number of presets that the user can call up, and these can either be used as they are or as a basis on which to create new effects, which can be saved for later use. Both factory presets and user memories can be called up via the front-panel controls, and MIDI program selection is supported on all but the cheapest units. Not only does this make it possible to access patches quickly but it also makes it possible to automatically change from one reverb setting to another during a mix by using a MIDI sequencer synchronised to the multitrack recorder. If there are more than 128 presets and user patches present on the equipment, these are normally organised into banks so that they can be accessed with MIDI Bank Change messages.

# Zipper Noise

MIDI may also be used to change some effect parameters in real time during a mix, usually under the control of a MIDI sequencer. However, there's a factor known as zipper noise that might become a problem, especially with older or cheaper models. When a value is changed within a digital-effect algorithm it is done so in a series of small discrete steps rather than continuously, as in the case of an analogue control knob. If these steps are big enough a change in parameters such as level, chorus depth, EQ or delay time may be accompanied by an fast and audible ticking known as zipper noise. More sophisticated units use a system known as linear interpolation to smooth out these steps, resulting in smoother parameter changes. The only way to avoid zipper noise when using cheaper units is to take advantage of any pauses in the music to make changes to the necessary parameters.

# Effects Patching

Effects such as reverb are normally fed from a post-fade send control (effects send), which means that the reverb level will increase and decrease with the original sound if the channel fader is moved. This is obviously the best way to work, though it's possible to drive a reverb unit from a pre-fade send if you want to fade out the dry signal while still leaving the reverb audible. This may prove useful in those situations when you want to create a special effect. The aux send system has the advantage that it allows the same effects device to be shared between all of the mixer channels while still allowing different amounts of effect on each channel. For example, you might be able to use the same reverb setting on both drums and vocals, but you may want to use more on the vocals than on the drums.

To maintain a stereo effect while mixing, the reverb left and right outputs should be panned hard left and right in the mix. A multitrack workstation with stereo effects returns will automatically pan the signals left and right, but if you're using spare input channels you'll have to do this manually.

If all of the effects sends are in use then effects may be connected via insert points, although in this case they can be used on that one channel only. When working in the aux send/return mode the dry sound should be turned off on the effects unit. When used via an insert point, the effect/dry balance must be set on the effects unit itself.

# Useful Facts

• Insert points are invariably presented as stereo jacks, wired to carry both the send and return signals, so if you don't have a patchbay you'll need a Y-lead with a stereo jack on one end and two monos on the other.

• If an effect is used via the aux/send return system, it's common practice to set the effects unit's dry/effect balance to effect only in order to allow the console's aux send controls to control the balance of effect.

- Some effects, such as phasing and flanging, rely on an effect/dry balance of some precision, which may be better accomplished on the effects unit itself. To achieve this, either patch the effects unit into an insert point, or, if you have to use the aux/send system, you can either de-route the channel from the stereo mix to kill the dry signal or feed the effects unit from a pre-fade (foldback) send and turn the channel fader right down.

- To use a mono in/stereo out effects unit (such as reverb or stereo delay) via insert points, simply route one output of the unit to the insert return of the channel feeding it and the other to the insert return of an adjacent channel. Match the levels, and then pan one track hard left and the other hard right for maximum stereo effect.

- To use a stereo in/stereo out effects unit via insert points use two adjacent mixer channels panned hard left and right.

## Multi-Effects Units

Every studio should have at least one good reverb processor, but after that the chances are that your effects will be produced by a multi-effects box which can turn its hand to any of the most popular studio effects, including delay, reverb and pitch shifting. It's even possible to use some multi-effects units as two almost independent effects units connected to separate console aux sends, but it's important to be aware that some of these devices share out their processing power between the different effects in different ways, and you may find that once you've managed to set up your ideal multi-effect arrangement on one channel there isn't enough power available to drive a really good reverb algorithm on the other.

Another consideration when using this type of effect is how you patch it into your system. Reverb is almost always fed directly from a post-fade aux send, but in the case of multi-effects that are being applied to just a single track it's sometimes a better idea to patch them into the channel insert point in order to avoid incurring any mix buss noise. Obviously, if you have a conventional dual channel effects box at your disposal it's only possible to use it one way or the other, not both.

# Backing Up Patches

Effects patches can take a long time to create, and because they're held in battery-powered internal RAM memory they can occasionally be corrupted by power surges or even fail altogether if the battery dies on you. These internal batteries last around five years on average, but when they do fail there's no warning: one day the unit is fine but the next your user patches have gone forever. ROM-based factory patches will remain, of course, but who uses only those? If you have a sequencer you back up your patch edits by doing a Sysex dump; restoring the patches is usually as simple as playing the sequence back into the effects unit, and it only takes a few seconds.

MIDI Sysex dumps also provide you with a means of downloading third-party patches into your machine, so if you have friends who use effects units which are the same models are your own then an hour or two spent swapping patches can be quite productive. Of course you can't load patches from a different make or model of unit, even if they appear to use the same basic parameters, because the system-exclusive commands are, as the name suggests, exclusive to individual machines.

# Multi-Effect Combinations

Though multi-effects units usually concentrate mainly on reverb, delay and pitch-based effects, many also contain components based on signal processors, such as mixers, equalisers, gates, compressors, exciters, speaker simulators, overdrive effects and even swept-resonant synth-style filters. A few units even include a vocoder, which is a device used to impose the frequency characteristics of one sound onto another via a frequency analyser and a filter bank.

Mixer modules are also included in this list because, within a multi-effects unit, the signal can generally be routed in many different ways through several combinations of effects blocks. Whenever it's necessary to mix together the outputs of two effects blocks, or when a dry signal has to be mixed with the output of an effects block, a mixing element is required. As far as the user is concerned it's usually only necessary to adjust levels, as the routing system automatically positions mixers wherever they are needed. When the output of one effects block is fed into the input of another (ie in a series connection) there is no need for a mixer, but when the outputs from two parallel effects blocks are combined a mixer will be required. Blocks may also incorporate mixing elements – for example, a delay block will require a mixer in order to balance the dry and delayed sound.

Simpler multi-effects units may be limited to connecting the various effects blocks in a series chain, and the simplest of these units place the blocks in a preset order, leaving the user with choice of which blocks to use and which to turn off. More sophisticated systems allow the user to rearrange the blocks into different orders, and it's quite common for both series and parallel connection to be permitted. Figure 6.3 shows both series and parallel routing options.

# Filters

Filters are often included under the umbrella of effects units, not only in the form of parametric and graphic equalisers but also as emulations of the swept-resonant filters used in synthesisers. The filter used in a typical analogue synthesiser is closely related to the parametric equaliser, the main difference being that, as well as being controlled by the user, the frequency of the filter can also be controlled electronically. For example, an

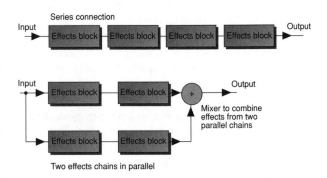

**Figure 6.3: Series and parallel routing options**

LFO could be used to sweep the frequency up and down, or an envelope could be generated to provide a filter sweep. You'll probably also find that the filter can be set to a higher Q; some go so high that they self resonate and turn into an oscillator. Some of the more sophisticated multi-effects processors include not only resonant-synth-type filters but also a variety of possible control sources, including envelopes derived from the input signal level, MIDI-triggered envelopes and LFOs.

# Processing Blocks

Gates are sometimes included in effects units to help remove the noise from hissy sound sources. Though not a complete solution to eradicating noise, gates can be useful when working with electric guitars, which often generate a lot of hiss and hum, especially when used with overdrive. Another studio processor that regularly shows up in multi-effects boxes is the compressor, the most popular use of which is in controlling vocal, drum and bass levels, although in a multi-effect unit they may also be used to add sustain to guitars, to reshape the decay characteristics of reverb decay or to compress the input or output of one of the other effects blocks. In other words, the compressor is more likely to be used in a creative rather than corrective mode when in a multi-effects environment. Because compressors increase the level of programme noise during quiet passages they are often used in conjunction with a gate. As a rule, the gate is usually linked up before the compressor.

Most stand-alone enhancers create a sense of brightness and transparency by manipulating the high-frequency end of the audio spectrum. Within a multi-effects unit, exciters may be used to brighten individual instruments, or, if the routing will permit it, they may be placed after another effects block to brighten one component of the sound – the output from a reverb or delay, for example.

# Amp/Speaker Simulators

While keyboards work best through a sound system with a flat frequency response and minimal distortion, guitar and bass amplifiers are voiced, which means that their frequency response is shaped to suit the instrument rather than left flat. Furthermore, the loudspeakers and enclosures used in guitar and bass amplification tend to have a very limited frequency response, which enables them to filter out the rougher components of amplifier distortion. If you were to DI a distorted guitar without EQ the result would be very thin and raspy compared to what you would hear from an amplifier. The amp/speaker simulator was devised to make DI'ing the guitar a more practical proposition, and this device includes a filter circuit that mimics the amplifier and speaker voicing of a typical guitar amp. Many multi-effects units now include amp/speaker simulators as well as overdrive, which enables the user to create a fully produced guitar sound within one unit, and the output may then be recorded without further processing. In addition to creating authentic miked guitar amp sounds, amp/speaker simulators are also useful for warming up digital synths where a fatter, more analogue sound is desired.

Guitar pre-amps and speaker simulators that operate with physical modelling can sound particularly authentic. However, even without this it's possible to produce a digital equivalent of an overdrive pedal, and that's what many multi-effects boxes provide. Serious guitarists may still want to use their own analogue distortion pedals before the multi-effects box, which is fine, but digital overdrive can also be used to great effect on organ and pad sounds if used in moderation. Drum sounds and loops may also be 'crunched' in interesting ways.

## Summary

Effects are essential in modern recording, and reverb is the most important of all. Fortunately good multi-effects units are now relatively cheap, but if you can only afford one unit then make sure it can deliver smooth, natural reverb as well as the more dramatic effects. Poor-quality reverb units have a metallic ring to them when percussive sounds are treated, such as snare drums. Software plug-ins are a viable alternative to hardware effects for the desktop studio, but your computer must be powerful enough to handle them along with the other functions.

# 7 SOFTWARE PLUG-INS

Once the sole domain of specialised hardware, many of the traditional recording and signal processing tasks are now available in software form, either using the native processing power of desktop Macs and PCs or running on DSP cards optimised for audio applications. The turning point, as far as home recording musicians were concerned, occurred when the major manufacturers of sequencers began adding audio recording, mixing and signal processing capabilities to their systems, which could be used with only the native processing power of the host computer. This had the result of opening up a whole world of recording to those musicians who previously might have been able to buy only a basic MIDI sequencing system.

For the more sophisticated user, who may need to run a number of powerful processing and mixing applications at the same time, even powerful desktop computers have insufficient processing power, especially when it's necessary to perform several processing jobs at the same time. The next stage is to use a computer system that uses DSP (Digital Signal Processing) cards, which are often plugged directly into the expansion slots of PCs and Macs. Although it's possible to use either cheap soundcards or the computer's own 16-bit analogue I/O ports to send and receive signals, high-quality external converters are preferable for use with serious applications as they tend to offer a better signal-to-noise performance and will probably support 24-bit operation.

# Third-Party Plug-ins

A range of plug-in effects and processing software is available from a number of third-party suppliers, which means that the functionality of the host software (for a example, an audio-plus-MIDI sequencer) may be expanded in various ways. Different versions may be required, however, depending on whether the host system runs on a Mac or PC and on whether the effects are to run on the native processor or on a DSP system. DSP chips are not generally compatible with those of a different design, and new generations of DSP are appearing all the time, so it's important to make sure that you buy the correct version of plug-in for your system. The most common standard for real-time plug-ins is currently VST (Virtual Studio Technology), which was created by Steinberg but was then opened up to all of the major music software companies in order to promote compatibility. VST plug-ins are available for both Mac and PC platforms, and are also supported by a great deal of third-party software.

# Native Plug-ins

The operation of native plug-ins relies entirely on the host computer's processor and memory, and the more plug-ins you want to run at the same time the more powerful a processor you will need. Some plug-ins require more processing power than others, and a good reverb package can use up a significant proportion of your overall processing resources. Sophisticated de-noising and de-clicking software is also processor intensive.

One way around having to buy a powerful processor is to use a non-real-time plug-in. These generally allow you to audition a short loop of audio, held in RAM while you adjust the various parameters. The whole audio file or section of file is then processed off-line. This will obviously take some time if you're using a slow computer. Unlike a real-time process that doesn't actually change the source audio file, off-line processes are destructive in that either the original file is changed or a new file is created reflecting the processing changes.

The plug-in will be deployed in different ways depending on the type of software package with which it is used.

For example, in a sophisticated MIDI-plus-audio sequencer that includes a virtual mixer, real-time effects may be patched in via virtual insert points or aux sends and returns, while processors may be connected via insert points in the usual way. In a simpler multitrack system or a stereo-editing package, however, plug-ins are more likely to be used to process whole audio files or sections of files. Whole files can often be processed non-destructively in real time, although the processing of sections or regions within a file can often only be carried out in a destructive fashion.

# Using Multiple Plug-ins

The advantages of using plug-in effects and processors are that there's no wiring to worry about, they don't take up any space in your studio and you don't need a patchbay to connect them. Furthermore, all of your settings will be saved along with the rest of your song data, so you don't even have to try and remember which effects you used or how much of each effect was added to each channel.

Some DSP-based systems, such as Digidesign's widely supported TDM platform, allow a single plug-in to provide multiple occurrences of the same processor, each with different settings. For example, you may be able to load in a compressor plug-in and then use six of those compressors in different channels of the virtual mixer, all optimised for different programme material. The number of occurrences that a plug-in that may be used at the same time is limited by the amount of DSP processing power and RAM available, though some manufacturers of plug-ins may also build a limit into their software. The more sophisticated systems on the market allow the installation of additional DSP cards on those occasions when more processing capability is needed.

# Types Of Plug-in

Virtually any effect or processor that can exist in hardware form can be used in a software environment, and indeed there are direct software equivalents of well-known compressors, equalisers, gates and reverb units, as well as any number of general-purpose equalisers, delays and other devices. Although digital emulations of specific analogue processors are not always entirely accurate, there are several digital processes that can be carried out more effectively as a computer plug-in, and not only because of the more sophisticated display and interfacing possibilities which are often provided by the computer.

In addition to the more obvious processes, plug-ins can also handle de-noising, de-clicking and other high-level tasks, such as the azimuth correction of analogue tape masters made on improperly aligned machines. There are plug-ins which emulate physical-modelling guitar-amp simulators, elaborate dithering systems for optimising bit reduction (used when converting 20-bit recordings to 16-bit CD masters), vocoders, and even those to add deliberate noise and crackle in order to simulate vinyl recordings. These latter devices are fashionable for making new recordings sound like vintage vinyl samples, and include such parameters as record speed, recording age, amount of surface damage and so on. Processes like surround-sound mixing and encoding are also available with the use of plug-ins, enabling a multi-channel audio workstation to handle sophisticated TV and film sound mixing.

The plug-in environment also allows a significant number of some of the more off-the-wall ideas to flourish, such as multiband fuzz boxes, unusual dynamic equalisers with user-adjustable compression curves and frequency points, and various interesting metering systems for viewing stereo image, phase and frequency content. There are also a number of packages available on the market which deal with matters such as pitch manipulation, including those which are designed to tune up imperfect vocal tracks, stereo width enhancers, 3D sound-positioning algorithms, many types of spectral enhancing devices and even systems that allow you to analyse the spectral content of commercial recordings and then automatically EQ your own recordings to have the same spectrum.

At the time of writing the majority of plug-ins are designed to be used within software recording and editing environments, but manufacturers of some digital mixers are already adding DSP to their products so that effects or processes from third-party designers can be created within the mixer. This can be only a good thing, as it provides more choice for the user and may be a way of offsetting the shortage of analogue insert points on a typical budget digital mixing console.

## The Computer Interface

The obvious advantage available with using software is that computers are able to provide an excellent graphic interface, and so plug-ins often provide dynamic graphs of compressor slopes, EQ curves and other criteria as well as controls and meters. Another positive factor is that computers don't have to do everything in real time. For example, if there is a process that could be completed more effectively if the computer could analyse the signal a little before processing it, then this is no problem: you could always delay the process for a fraction of a second so that the algorithm could scan ahead to check out the material coming along. The whole sound file can be scanned prior to being processed, a process which proves necessary for procedures such as normalisation, where the gain of the entire file is adjusted so that the very loudest peak coincides with odB FS (Full Scale).

# Plug-in Automation

It's a well-known fact that MIDI effects units may have some of their parameters automated by the use of MIDI controller information, but there are many plug-ins on the market that may now also be automated, including the popular VST range. While it's true that some processes don't lend themselves to automation in any obvious way, effects such as delay, reverb or even guitar amp simulation can be automated in this way to produce some very creative mixes.

# Computing Power

Having effects that can run in real time on a host computer with no additional hardware other than a simple soundcard is clearly very attractive, but despite the ever-increasing performance of computers, users always seem to demand a level of performance one step ahead of what technology can comfortably offer. At least real effects units can be used all at once if necessary without triggering a DSP overload error, but in the virtual domain you'll come up against a limit somewhere or other. Good-quality reverb is particularly DSP hungry, so a number of systems have been developed in which the soundcard includes a dedicated reverb processor to take off some of the load from the host processor. This seems to be an effective approach, and one that other manufacturers may follow. It has the advantage that dedicated reverb engines may be used to provide better-quality reverb than that which would normally be available from a host-processor-driven system, and it frees up the power of the host processor to be used for other effects or processes. As far as the software is concerned, both the hardware reverb and the virtual effects are accessed in the same way.

# 8 MIXING WITH EFFECTS

Effects and processors can either make or break a mix, so it's just as important to know when to use them as it is to know how to use them. For me, the most rewarding part of any project the final mix, and it's at this stage of the proceedings that effects and signal processors can be used to turn a simple recording into a major production. It's here that the temptation to overdo things must be resisted, as it's very easy to spoil the end result by turning it into a special-effects circus. Following these guidelines will introduce you to the safe way of using effects, but once you've learnt the basics it's worth breaking a few rules just to see what happens.

When setting up a mix, try to get it sounding as near perfect as possible before adding any effects or signal processing. Check the sound and overall balance against a familiar record, and also check that the balance sounds right when you're standing outside the room with the door open (this is a very revealing test used by many professionals). When you've got the general balance right, add further vocal compression if necessary so that the vocals sit comfortably with the backing track. Once you're happy with the overall timbre and balance, adding effects 'for effect' should be easier. Remember that, in most cases, effects are used just to add the final gloss; they won't compensate for a poor balance or bad basic sounds. Don't be tempted to hide poor playing by heaping on more effects; it never works – take it from one who's tried everything at one time or another! However, thanks to the wonders of modern technology, slightly imperfect vocal pitching can be tightened up almost magically with some of the better hardware or software pitch-correction processors.

Reverb is the most important of all effects, and so is probably the next thing to add, after you've got a decent balance on the mixer and fine-tuned the EQ. Reverb creates the illusion of space, but in doing so it also smears the stereo localisation of the original sound source, just as it does in real life. If you want to maintain a specific stereo placement for one or more sounds in a mix, consider using a mono reverb effect and panning the reverb to the same position as the original dry sound.

Vocal reverb is particularly important, as it makes the vocals sound more musical and helps them sit with the rest of the mix, although adding too much will have the effect of pushing the vocals back rather than allowing them to take their position at the front of the mix. Experiment with pre-delay values of 60–100ms to help counteract this, and also try using a reverb patch that has a lot of early reflections, as these will help to reinforce the dry sound. You can learn a lot from listening carefully to other records to hear how much and what type of reverb were used. You'll often find that you need to add rather less than you'd though.

Bright vocal reverbs are fashionable but may exaggerate sibilance. As an alternative to de-essing the vocals, try instead de-essing just the feed to the reverb unit so that only the effected part of the signal is treated. Always use your best reverb unit for vocals, as it's here that the biggest differences are audible. Don't compromise by using a poor-quality software reverb plug-in just because you're short of processing power; use a good external hardware reverb unit if you have one, or choose a more powerful software plug-in to treat the vocal track in non-real time. This may mean off-line processing or carrying out a real-time 'bounce to disk' of the vocal track in isolation via the plug-in.

Don't add long reverb to bass sounds unless you have an artistic reason to do so, as this tends to muddy the low end of the mix. If you need to add space to a kick drum, try using a short ambience program or a gated reverb as an alternative. If you're in a position where you need to apply reverb to an entire drum mix, try rolling off the low end feeding the reverb to arrive at a cleaner sound.

# Dynamics

Pop vocals invariably require compression. Rather than applying all of the compression at the recording stage, however, it's best to apply a little less than you think you might ultimately need and then add more when you come to mix. This dual-stage process ensures that you don't record an over-compressed sound, and it also helps to even out the level of the recorded signal. Different models of compressor produce different sounds, so use the one that has the most flattering effect on the vocal with which you're working. As a rule, opto and tube compressors produce the warmest, most solid sound.

Unfortunately, compressors bring up low-level noise just as effectively as they bring up low-level signals, so you might try gating the signal prior to compression when you're mixing. You should also use no more compression than you need to avoid unnecessarily compromising the signal-to-noise ratio. However, it's

## basic Effects & Processors

usually unwise to gate the compressor input during recording because, if the gate is set up badly, you'll ruin an otherwise good take. It's better to gate while mixing, when you have the opportunity to reset the parameters, and then try again if it doesn't work out the first time. A further benefit is that any noise, crosstalk or spill accumulated during recording will also be gated out.

Always gate signals prior to adding reverb or delay where possible, as gates can easily chop off the tail end of a long reverb or echo. Furthermore, if you add reverb or echo after gating then any minor gating side-effects, such as shortened notes, will probably be completely hidden by the natural decay of the reverb or echo. Any noise added to the mix by the reverb unit should be negligible, as long as you've paid attention to the structure and level setting of the gain when adjusting the effects.

Don't always set your gates to fully attenuate the signal when the gate is closed. In some situations it may sound more natural if a low level of background noise is still audible between wanted sounds, and when working with drums you'll find that the gate opens faster if the range control is set to around 12dB rather than to maximum.

# Minimising Noise

Single-ended noise-reduction units (the type that work by applying level-dependent top cut) can be very useful in reducing the perceived level of hiss with material in which there are no silences that would trigger a gate or expander to operate. However, you should make constant comparisons to ensure that there's no obvious top-end loss when the unit is switched on. If there is then lower the threshold slightly until there is an acceptable compromise between high-end loss during low-level passages and audible hiss. As with gates, applying reverb after dynamic filtering will help disguise any side-effects as well as safeguard the reverb tails from being truncated. I find that single-ended noise-reduction units are particularly effective at cleaning up electric guitar sounds, though they won't help remove low-frequency hum.

# EQ As An Effect

Because every channel of a mixing desk has EQ controls we tend to take it for granted, but EQ is a signal-processing function like any other. Equalisation is often seen as an alternative to recording a good-quality sound at source, but the result is seldom as satisfactory as recording a sound as accurately as possible. Nevertheless, on those occasions when equalisation is necessary, applying cut to the over-emphasised frequencies rather than boost to weaker ones generally results in a more natural sound, especially with vocals and acoustic instruments. This is especially true of on-desk equalisers or budget parametric equalisers, as they often sound nasal or phasey when used to boost mid-range sounds. If you can afford it, buy at least one good outboard reverb for those occasions when you come across something tricky that requires a lot of EQ. As you might imagine, natural sounds, such as voices and acoustic instruments, suffer most from poor-quality equalisation.

Sounds can often be made to sit better in a mix by bracketing them with high- and low-pass filters to restrict their spectral content. Many console EQs don't have the sharp filters needed to do this, but the side-chain filters fitted to many gates are often ideal for the job. Simply set the gate to its Side-Chain Listen mode and then use the filters to shave away unwanted high and low frequencies. Acoustic guitars often work better in a mix if the low end is rolled off in this way, though the high end can usually be left alone.

# Enhancement Effects

Chorus is a useful effect for creating or enhancing the illusion of space and movement, but it also tends to push sounds back in the mix, in much the same way as reverb. If you need a sound treated with chorus to stand out in a mix, either try panning a dry version of the sound to one side and a chorused version to the other or ensure that the song's arrangement leaves plenty of room for the chorused sound. Creating chorus by using a pitch shifter to set up a slight detuning effect, combined with the dry sound, can sound less obviously cyclic than conventional chorus. If you have a two-voice pitch shifter, try setting up two shifted signals, one a little sharp and the other flat. Again, add the original signal and pan the shifted signals to either side to obtain more width and movement.

Take additional care when using high-frequency enhancers to treat complex mixes as your ears can soon get used to the effect, and you may end up adding more than is desirable. Make frequent use of the bypass button to remind you just how radically the sound has changed, and if you're adding more than a little high-end enhancement then check the bottom end to determine if it needs bringing up in order to keep the mix in balance. It's often better to enhance just a few elements of mix to make them stand out from the rest. The best way to do this is to connect the enhancer to the a pair of group insert points and then send all of the sounds that need enhancing to that group. Listen carefully to enhanced vocals, as the process can often exaggerate problems with sibilance.

Treatments designed to increase the stereo width of a mix (other than the simple trick of mixing antiphase signals into the opposite channel) can have detrimental effects on mono compatibility. It's important to use your console's mono button to check that your mix doesn't lose too much when it's played in mono because the material may be played over mono radios or TVs, so listen out for the subjective balance or timbre changing too much. If it does, either use less overall width expansion or leave the main mix elements untreated and only process secondary sounds, such as incidental percussion, sound effects, effects returns and so on.

# Bass And Drum Treatments

Bass guitars, kick drums and other low-frequency sound sources should generally be panned to the centre of the mix so that the heavy load of the bass frequencies can be shared equally by the two speakers in a stereo system. As a rule, low-frequency sounds don't provide strong auditory clues as to direction, so panning bass sounds to the centre isn't too much of a restriction. If you want to add stereo movement to an instrument like a fretless bass, adding a stereo chorus (or a mono chorus panned to one side and the dry sound to the other) will usually do the trick while still spreading the load between the two speakers reasonably evenly. Always check stereo effects in mono, as some may become sound much less pronounced and some older devices may actually cancel them out altogether. Although most new sound systems are stereo models, mono compatibility is still an important issue for music destined to be heard over mono TVs or transistor radios.

Bass guitars often need to be compressed to keep their level under control, and even if you've already compressed during recording there's no reason not to compress even more when you mix. Just bear in mind that, in adding more compression, you'll also be bringing up more background noise. It may therefore be a good idea to gate the bass before compressing it further. The attack of the bass sound can be modified after recording to some extent by adjusting the compressor's attack time. Also, ensure that the release time is just as fast – this can be done without the level pumping unacceptably.

You'll need an equaliser to change the tonality of a bass guitar, but you're more likely to get better results with a multiband parametric or even a good graphic equaliser than you are with the EQ on your desk. Don't waste too much time trying to get a great bass sound in isolation, however, as it'll almost certainly sound quite different when the rest of the mix is up. In fact, there's a good argument for not equalising anything until you have a reasonable rough balance set up. If you think that the bass lacks punch, a little boost at 80–100Hz should help.

If the bass sound comes from a synth or a sampler then compression is unlikely to be necessary, though you can EQ the sound in just the same way as you would the real instrument. The same applies to effects, but you should still use effects sparingly on bass sounds.

# Drums In The Mix

Drum sounds are very much a matter of personal taste and are influenced by musical fashions, but it's fair to say that few contemporary styles require that a recorded drum kit sounds exactly like its acoustic counterpart. Exceptions to this rule include jazz and indie music, where more recognisable drum sounds are appropriate.

Gating can be used to tighten and separate the sound if the drums have been close miked and are recorded on separate tracks. A compressor with a medium attack time or a transient enhancer can be used to add more snap to the individual drum sounds, and of course EQ can be employed to add punch or remove boxiness. Boost applied between 80–120Hz adds weight, while a little 6kHz boost will sharpen up the attack. Boxy toms can be tamed by pulling back at 200–150Hz, and air can be added to the whole kit by boosting the overhead mics at around 15kHz, using a low Q setting. A harmonic enhancer can also help brighten up a dull drum sound.

Snare drums are interesting because no two are quite the same. The type of drum will define its basic sound, so it's no good expecting a deep, woody, heavy metal sound from a metal piccolo snare, or a metallic ring from a deep wood shell model, for that matter. You can cheat a little by adding depth to snare drums or kick drums by using a pitch shifter, but as a rule the drum sound is largely defined at source. If the sound of the snare or kick drum turns out to be inappropriate and you can't persuade the drummer to play it again, try gating it and using the gated signal to trigger a sampler or drum machine, as explained earlier in the book.

You'll need a decent reverb to treat drums, but don't feel that you have to add a lot of reverb because most drums don't need it – just add enough to create a sense of space. Plate settings have always been the mainstay of drum treatments, but with today's eclectic music you can use whatever is artistically appropriate. It makes sense to avoid adding much in the way of reverb to kick drums and other low percussion sounds, however, as this tends to muddy the mix. If muddiness is a problem, try rolling off some low end from the reverb send or return.

# APPENDIX
# Common Cable Connections

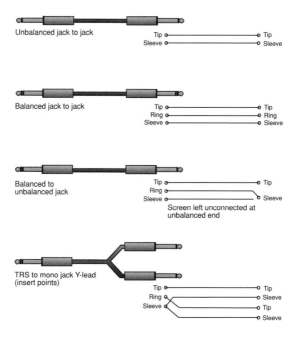

Unbalanced jack to jack

Tip o————————o Tip
Sleeve o————————o Sleeve

Balanced jack to jack

Tip o————————o Tip
Ring o————————o Ring
Sleeve o————————o Sleeve

Balanced to
unbalanced jack

Tip o————————o Tip
Ring o————————
Sleeve o————————o Sleeve

Screen left unconnected at
unbalanced end

TRS to mono jack Y-lead
(insert points)

Tip o————————o Tip
Ring o————————o Sleeve
Sleeve o————————o Tip
————————o Sleeve

## basic Effects & Processors

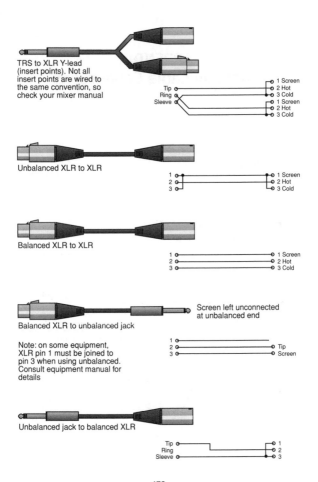

TRS to XLR Y-lead
(insert points). Not all
insert points are wired to
the same convention, so
check your mixer manual

Tip
Ring
Sleeve

1 Screen
2 Hot
3 Cold
1 Screen
2 Hot
3 Cold

Unbalanced XLR to XLR

1
2
3

1 Screen
2 Hot
3 Cold

Balanced XLR to XLR

1
2
3

1 Screen
2 Hot
3 Cold

Balanced XLR to unbalanced jack

Screen left unconnected
at unbalanced end

Note: on some equipment,
XLR pin 1 must be joined to
pin 3 when using unbalanced.
Consult equipment manual for
details

1
2
3

Tip
Screen

Unbalanced jack to balanced XLR

Tip
Ring
Sleeve

1
2
3

# GLOSSARY

## Active
Describes a circuit containing transistors, ICs, tubes and other devices that require power to operate and are capable of amplification.

## ADSR
Envelope generator with Attack, Decay, Sustain and Release parameters. This is a simple type of envelope generator and was first used on early analogue synthesisers, though similar envelopes may be found in some effects units to control filter sweeps and suchlike.

## AFL
After-Fade Listen, a system used within mixing consoles to allow specific signals to be monitored at the level set by their fader or level control knob. Aux sends are generally monitored AFL rather than PFL so that the actual signal being fed to an effects unit can be monitored.

## Aftertouch
Means of generating a control signal based on how

much pressure is applied to the keys of a MIDI keyboard. Most instruments that support this do not have independent pressure sensing for all keys but detect the overall pressure on a sensing strip running beneath the keys. Aftertouch may be used to control vibrato depth, filter brightness, loudness and so on, though it may also be used to control some parameter of a MIDI effects unit, such as delay feedback or effect level.

# Algorithm

Computer program designed to perform a specific task. In the context of effects units, algorithms usually describe a software building block designed to create a specific effect or combination of effects. All digital effects are based on algorithms.

# Ambience

Addition of sound reflections in a confined space to the original sound. Ambience may also be created electronically by some digital reverb units. Ambience and reverberation are different in that ambience doesn't have the characteristic long delay time of reverberation – the reflections mainly give the sound a sense of space.

# Amplifier

Device that increases the level of an electrical signal.

# Amplitude

Another word for level. Can refer to sound or electrical signal.

# Analogue

Describes circuitry that uses a continually changing voltage or current to represent a signal. The origin of the term is that the electrical signal can be thought of as being analogous to the original signal.

# Attack

Time taken for a sound to achieve maximum amplitude. Drums have a fast attack, whereas bowed strings have a slow attack. In compressors and gates, the attack time equates to how quickly the processor can change its gain.

# Attenuate

To make lower in level.

# Aux

Control on a mixing console designed to route some of the channel signal to the effects or cue mix outputs (see *Aux Send*).

# Aux Return

Mixer inputs used to add effects to the mix.

# Aux Send

Physical output from a mixer aux send buss.

# Balance

This word has several meanings in recording. It may refer to the relative levels of the left and right channels of a stereo recording, or it may be used to describe the relative levels of the various instruments and voices within a mix.

# Balanced Wiring

Wiring system which uses two out-of-phase conductors and a common screen to reduce the effect of interference. For balancing to be effective, both the sending and receiving device must have balanced output and input stages respectively.

# Bandpass Filter

Filter that removes or attenuates frequencies above and below a set frequency. Frequencies within the band are emphasised. They are often used in synthesisers as tone-shaping elements.

# Bandwidth

Means of specifying the range of frequencies passed by an electronic circuit such as an amplifier, mixer or filter. The frequency range is usually measured at the points where the level drops by 3dB relative to the maximum.

## Boost/Cut Control

Control which allows the range of frequencies passing through a filter to be either amplified or attenuated. The centre position is usually the 'flat' or 'no effect' position.

## Bouncing

Process of mixing two or more recorded tracks together and re-recording these onto another track.

## Buss

Common electrical signal path along which signals may travel. In a mixer, there are several busses carrying the stereo mix, the groups, the PFL signal, the aux sends and so on. Power supplies are also fed along busses.

## Channel

There are 16 data channels over which MIDI data may be sent. The organisation of data by channels means that up to 16 MIDI instruments or parts may be addressed using one cable.

## Channel

In the context of mixing consoles, a channel is a single strip of controls relating to one input.

# Chorus

Effect created by doubling a signal and adding delay and pitch modulation.

# Clipping

Severe form of distortion which occurs when a signal attempts to exceed the maximum level a piece of equipment can handle.

# Compressor

Device designed to reduce the dynamic range of audio signals by reducing the level of high signals or by increasing the level of low signals.

# Conductor

Material that provides a low resistance path for electrical current.

# Console

Alternative term for mixer.

# Cut-Off Frequency

Frequency above or below which attenuation begins in a filter circuit.

# Cycle

One complete vibration of a sound source or its

electrical equivalent. One cycle per second is expressed as one Hertz (Hz).

## Damping

With reverb, this refers to the rate at which reverberant energy is absorbed by the surfaces in an environment.

## DAT

Digital Audio Tape. The most commonly used DAT machines are more correctly known as R-DATs because they use a rotating head similar to that in a video recorder. Digital recorders using fixed or stationary heads (such as DCC) are known as S-DAT machines.

## dB

Decibel. Unit used to express the relative levels of two electrical voltages, powers or sounds.

## dbx

A commercial encode/decode tape noise reduction system that compresses the signal during recording and expands it by an identical amount on playback.

## DCC

Stationary-head digital recorder format developed by Philips. Uses a data-compression system to reduce the amount of data that needs to be stored.

# DDL
Digital Delay Line.

# Decay
Progressive reduction in amplitude of a sound or electrical signal over time. In the context of an Attack/Decay/Sustain/Release envelope shaper, the decay phase starts as soon as the attack phase has reached its maximum level. In the decay phase, the signal level drops until it reaches the sustain level set by the user. The signal then remains at this level until the key is released, at which point the release phase is entered.

# De-esser
Device for reducing the effect of sibilance in signals which include vocals.

# DI
Direct Inject, in which a signal is plugged directly into an audio chain without the aid of a microphone.

# DI Box
Device for matching the signal-level impedance of a source to a tape machine or mixer input.

# Digital

Electronic system which represents data and signals in the form of codes comprising 1s and 0s.

# Digital Delay

Digital processor for generating delay and echo effects.

# Digital Reverb

Digital processor for simulating reverberation.

# DIN Connector

Consumer multipin signal connection format, also used for MIDI cabling. Various pin configurations are available.

# Dither

System of adding low-level noise to a digitised audio signal in such a way that extends the low-level resolution at the expense of a slight deterioration in noise performance.

# Dry

Signal to which no effects have been added. Conversely, a sound which has been treated with an effect, such as reverberation, is referred to as wet.

# DSP

Digital Signal Processor. A powerful microchip used to process digital signals.

# Ducking

System for controlling the level of one audio signal with another. For example, background music can be made to duck whenever there is a voice-over.

# Dump

To transfer digital data from one device to another. A Sysex dump is a means of transmitting information about a particular instrument or module over MIDI, and may be used to store sound patches, parameter settings and so on.

# Dynamic Range

Range in decibels between the highest signal that can be handled by a piece of equipment and the level at which small signals disappear into the noise floor.

# Dynamics

Method of describing the relative levels within a piece of music.

# Early Reflections

First sound reflections from walls, floors and ceilings following a sound created in an acoustically reflective environment.

# Effects Loop

Connection system that allows an external signal processor to be connected into the audio chain.

# Effects Return

Additional mixer input designed to accommodate the output from an effects unit.

# Effects Unit

Device for treating an audio signal in order to change it in some creative way. Effects often involve the use of delay circuits, and include such treatments as reverb and echo.

# Enhancer

Device which brightens audio material by using techniques like dynamic equalisation, phase shifting and harmonic generation.

# Envelope

How the level of a sound or signal varies over time.

# Equaliser

Device for cutting or boosting parts of the audio spectrum.

# Exciter

Enhancer that synthesises new high-frequency harmonics.

# Expander
Device designed to decrease the level of low-level signals and increase the level of high-level signals, thus increasing the dynamic range of the signal.

# Fader
Sliding potentiometer control used in mixers and other processors.

# File
Meaningful list of data stored in digitally. A Standard MIDI File is a specific type of file designed to allow sequence information to be exchanged between different types of sequencer.

# Filter
Electronic circuit designed to emphasise or attenuate a specific range of frequencies.

# Flanging
Modulated delay effect using feedback to create a dramatic, sweeping sound.

# Foldback
System for feeding one or more separate mixes to the performers for use while recording and overdubbing. Also known as a *cue mix*.

# Formant
Characteristic resonance that doesn't change in proportion pitch. For example, the body resonance of an acoustic guitar.

# Frequency
Indication of how many cycles of a repetitive waveform occur in one second. A waveform which has a repetition cycle of once per second has a frequency of 1Hz.

# Frequency Response
Measurement of the range of frequencies that can be handled by a specific piece of electrical equipment or a loudspeaker.

# Fundamental
Any sound comprises a fundamental or basic frequency plus harmonics and partials at a higher frequency.

# Gain
Amount by which a circuit amplifies a signal.

# Gate
Electrical signal generated when a key is depressed on an electronic keyboard. This is used to trigger envelope generators and other events that must be synchronised to key action.

# Gate

Electronic device which mutes low-level signals, thus improving the noise performance during pauses in the wanted material.

# Graphic Equaliser

Equaliser on which several narrow segments of the audio spectrum are controlled by individual cut/boost faders. The name derives from the fact that the fader positions provide a graphic representation of the EQ curve.

# Ground

Electrical earth, or zero volts. In mains wiring, the ground cable is connected to the ground via a long conductive metal spike.

# Ground Loops

Also known as *earth loops*. Wiring problem in which currents circulate in the ground wiring of an audio system, known as the ground loop effect. When these currents are induced by the alternating mains supply, hum results.

# Group

Collection of signals within a mixer that are mixed and then routed through a separate fader to provide overall control. In a multitrack mixer, several groups are provided to feed the various recorder track inputs.

# Hard Disk

High-capacity computer storage device based on a rotating rigid disk with a magnetic coating onto which data may be recorded.

# Harmonic

High-frequency component of a complex waveform.

# Head

Part of a tape machine or disk drive that reads and/or writes data to and from the storage media.

# Headroom

The safety margin in decibels between the highest peak signal being passed by a piece of equipment and the absolute maximum level the equipment can handle.

# High-Pass Filter

Filter which attenuates frequencies below its cut-off frequency.

# Hiss

Noise caused by random electrical fluctuations.

# Hum
Signal contamination caused by the addition of low frequencies, usually related to the mains power frequency.

# Hz
Shorthand for *hertz*, the unit of frequency.

# Inductor
Reactive component which presents an impedance with increases with frequency.

# Insert Point
Connector that allows an external processor to be patched into a signal path so that the signal then flows through the external processor.

# I/O
The part of a system that handles inputs and outputs, usually in the digital domain.

# Jack
Commonly used audio connector. Can be either mono (TS) or stereo (TRS).

# Limiter
Device that controls the gain of a signal so as to prevent

it from exceeding a preset level. A limiter is essentially a fast-acting compressor with an infinite compression ratio.

## Linear
Device where the output is a direct multiple of the input.

## Line Level
Mixers and signal processors tend to work at a standard signal level known as line level. In practice there are several different standard line levels, but all are in the order of a few volts. A nominal signal level is around −10dBv for semi-pro equipment and +4dBv for professional equipment.

## Low-Frequency Oscillator (LFO)
Oscillator used as a modulation source, usually below 20Hz. The most common waveshape is the sine wave, though there is often a choice between sine, square, triangular and sawtooth waves.

## Low-Pass Filter (LPF)
Filter that attenuates frequencies above its cut-off frequency.

## Mic Level
Low-level signal generated by a microphone. This must be amplified many times to increase it to line level.

# MIDI
Musical Instrument Digital Interface.

# MIDI Bank Change
Type of controller message used to select alternate banks of MIDI programs where access to more than 128 programs is required.

# MIDI Controller
Term used to describe the physical interface by which the musician plays the MIDI synthesiser or other sound generator. Examples include keyboards, drum pads and wind synths.

# (Standard) MIDI File
Standard file format for storing data recorded on a MIDI sequencer so it can be read by other models of sequencer.

# MIDI Note On/Off
Messages sent when a key is pressed and released respectively.

# Monitor
Reference loudspeaker used for mixing, or a computer screen. Also means the action of listening to a mix or audio signal.

# Monophonic
One note at a time.

# Multitrack
Device capable of recording several parts or tracks that may then be mixed or re-recorded independently.

# Noise Reduction
System for reducing analogue tape noise or for reducing the level of hiss present in a recording.

# Non-Linear Recording
Describes digital recording systems that allow any parts of the recording to be played back in any order with no gaps. Conventional tape is referred to as linear, because the material can only play back in the order in which it was recorded.

# Normalise
A socket is said to be normalised when it's wired so that the original signal path is maintained, unless a plug is inserted into the socket. The most common examples of normalised connectors are a mixing console's insert points.

# Octave
When a frequency or pitch is transposed up by one octave, its frequency is doubled.

# Offline

Process carried out while a recording is not playing. Some computer-based processes have to be carried out off-line as the computer isn't fast enough to carry out the process in real time.

# Oscillator

Circuit designed to generate a periodic electrical waveform.

# Pad

Resistive circuit for reducing signal level.

# Pan Pot

Control enabling the user of a mixer to move the signal to any point in the stereo soundstage by varying the relative levels that are fed to the left and right stereo outputs.

# Parallel

Method of connecting two or more circuits together so that their inputs and outputs are all connected together.

# Parametric EQ

Equaliser with controls for frequency, bandwidth and cut/boost.

# Patch Bay

System of panel-mounted connectors used to bring inputs and outputs to a central point from where they can be routed using plug-in patch cords.

# Peak

Maximum instantaneous level of a signal, or the highest signal level in any section of programme material.

# PFL

Pre-Fade Listen, a system used within a mixing console to allow the user to listen to a selected signal, regardless of the position of the fader controlling the signal.

# Phase

Timing difference between two electrical waveforms expressed in degrees, where 360 degrees corresponds to a delay of one cycle.

# Phaser

Effect which combines a signal with a phase-shifted version of itself to produce creative filtering effects. Most phasers are controlled by means of an LFO.

# Pick-up

Part of a guitar that converts string vibrations to electrical signals.

# Pitch Shifter

Device for changing the pitch of an audio signal without changing its duration.

# Post-Fade

Aux signal taken from after the channel fader so that the aux send level follows any channel fader changes. Normally used for feeding effects devices.

# Pre-Fade

Aux signal taken from before the channel fader so that the channel fader has no effect on the aux-send level. Pre-fade is normally used for creating foldback or cue mixes.

# Preset

Effects unit or synth patch that cannot be altered by the user.

# Processor

Device designed to treat an audio signal by changing its dynamics or frequency content. Examples of processors include compressors, gates and equalisers.

# Q

Measurement of the resonant properties of a filter. The higher the Q value, the more resonant the filter and the narrower the range of frequencies that are allowed to pass.

# Real Time
Audio process that can be carried out as the signal is being recorded or played back. The opposite is off-line, where the signal is processed in non-real time.

# Release
Time taken for a level or gain to return to normal. Often used to describe the rate at which a synthesised sound reduces in level after a key has been released.

# Resistance
Opposition to the flow of electrical current, measured in ohms.

# Resonance
Same as Q.

# Reverb
Acoustic effect created by reflections in a confined space.

# RMS
Root Mean Square. A method of specifying the behaviour of a piece of electrical equipment under continuous sine wave testing conditions.

# Sampling

Process carried out by an A/D converter where the instantaneous amplitude of a signal is measured many times per second (44.1kHz in the case of CD-quality material). The term also defines a digitised sound used as a musical sound source in a sampler or additive synthesiser.

# Sequencer

Device for recording and replaying MIDI data, usually in a multitrack format, allowing complex compositions to be built up a part at a time.

# Sibilance

High-frequency whistling or lisping that affects vocal recordings due to either poor mic technique or excessive equalisation.

# Side Chain

Part of a circuit that splits off a proportion of the main signal so that it can be processed in some way. Compressors use a side-chain signal to derive their control signals.

# Signal Chain

Route taken by a signal from the input of a system to its output.

## Signal-To-Noise Ratio

Ratio of maximum signal level to residual noise, measured in decibels.

## Stereo

Two-channel system feeding left and right loudspeakers.

## Sweet Spot

Best position for a mic or listener relative to monitor speakers.

## Sync

System designed to allow two or more pieces of equipment run in synchronism with each other.

## Synthesiser

Electronic musical instrument designed to create a wide range of sounds, both imitative and abstract.

## Timbre

Tonal 'colour' of a sound.

## TRS Jack

Stereo-type jack with tip, ring and sleeve connections.

## Unbalanced

Describes a two-wire electrical signal connection where

the inner (hot or positive) conductor is usually surrounded by the cold (negative) conductor, therefore forming a screen against interference.

# Vibrato
Pitch modulation using an LFO to modulate a VCO.

# XLR
Type of connector commonly used to carry balanced audio signals, including the feeds from microphones.

# Y-Lead
Lead split so that one source can feed two destinations. Y-leads may also be used in console insert points, when a stereo jack plug at one end of the lead is split into two monos at the other.

# Zipper Noise
Audible steps that occur when a parameter is being varied in a digital audio processor.